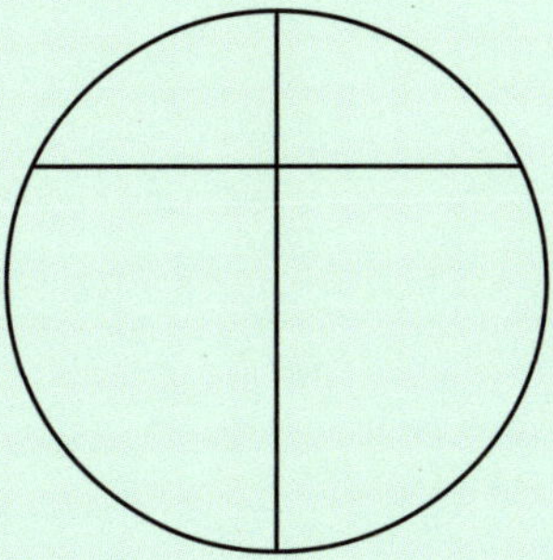

365 DAILY DEVOTIONALS

Christian Wisdom for Modern Life

JOANNA GRAY

Quadrille

CONTENTS

INTRODUCTION

The words within this devotional come from the minds, the mouths and the pens, of men and women across many centuries. Saints and sinners, whose lives had been elevated to a spiritual glory so powerful they were compelled to share their divine insights with the world. This small book is the latest in a golden chain of wisdom from those moved by the life and love of Jesus Christ.

This book does not follow the traditional ecclesiastical year, but instead offers a gentle introduction for a life leaning towards God. It begins with ways of approaching the Bible and prayer, before following the life of Christ, and contemplating issues that continue to challenge us today.

NOTE: SOME OF THE ARCHAIC LANGUAGE OF THE ANCIENT SAINTS AND MEDIEVAL MYSTICS HAS BEEN MODERNIZED TO MAKE IT EASIER TO READ.

1 JANUARY

MORNING

"In the beginning God created the heavens and the earth. The earth was without form, and void; and darkness was on the face of the deep. And the Spirit of God was hovering over the face of the waters.

Then God said, 'Let there be light'; and there was light. And God saw the light, that it was good; and God divided the light from the darkness. God called the light Day, and the darkness He called Night. So the evening and the morning were the first day."

GENESIS, CHAPTER 1, VERSES 1–5, NEW KING JAMES VERSION

Is it possible learn by heart the moment God spoke the universe into being?

"While the morning stars sang together and all the angels shouted for joy."

JOB, CHAPTER 38, VERSE 7, NEW INTERNATIONAL VERSION

I arise today, through
The strength of heaven,
The light of the sun,
The radiance of the moon,
The splendour of fire,
The speed of lightning,
The swiftness of wind,
The depth of the sea,
The stability of the earth,
The firmness of rock.

From the *Breastplate of Saint Patrick,* a 5th-century Romano-British saint. This prayer is a *lorica,* a Celtic prayer of protection.

4 JANUARY

"Receive every day as a resurrection from death, as a new enjoyment of life."

WILLIAM LAW, ENGLISH PRIEST

"O my God! I offer you all my actions of this day for the intentions and for the glory of the sacred heart of Jesus. I desire to sanctify every beat of my heart, my every thought, my simplest works, by uniting them to Jesus's infinite merits; and I wish to make reparation for my sins by casting them into the furnace of Jesus's merciful Love."

SAINT THÉRÈSE OF LISIEUX, FRENCH NUN

"Let go of your plans. The first hour of your morning belongs to God. Tackle the day's work that he charges you with, and he will give you the power to accomplish it."

SAINT TERESA BENEDICTA OF THE CROSS, CARMELITE NUN

Sometimes all we can manage is the contemplation of a few words. Use a single line from scripture as a repeated method of asking God to draw near.

"Sing to the Lord, all you godly ones!
Praise his holy name.
For his anger lasts only a moment,
but his favour lasts a lifetime!
Weeping may last through the night,
but joy comes with the morning."

PSALM 30, VERSES 4–5, NEW LIVING TRANSLATION

"Joy comes with the morning"

Such a beautiful sentiment bears repeating at the start of every day.

"Joy comes with the morning"

"O Lord who has brought us through the darkness of night to the light of morning, and by your Holy Spirit lightens the darkness of ignorance and sin: we ask you with your loving kindness to pour your holy light into our souls, so we may always be devoted to you."

BOOK OF HOURS – A MEDIEVAL CHRISTIAN SELF-HELP BOOK.

"For to us a child is born, to us a son is given, and the government will be on his shoulders. And he will be called Wonderful Counsellor, Mighty God, Everlasting Father, Prince of Peace."

ISAIAH, CHAPTER 9, VERSE 6, NEW INTERNATIONAL VERSION

Neither a god of thunderbolts, nor a god of war, the Christian God manifests as a tiny babe in arms. Today, reflect on all that is vulnerable and precious and imbued with the divine.

My soul doth magnify the Lord, and my spirit hath rejoiced in God my Saviour.

For He hath regarded the low estate of His handmaiden; for behold, from henceforth all generations shall call me blessed.

For He that is mighty hath done to me great things, and holy is His name; and His mercy is on them that fear Him from generation to generation.

He hath shewed strength with His arm; He hath scattered the proud in the imagination of their hearts.

He hath put down the mighty from their seats, and exalted them of low degree.

He hath filled the hungry with good things, and the rich He hath sent empty away.

He hath holpen His servant Israel in remembrance of His mercy, as He spake to our fathers, to Abraham and to his seed for ever.

Glory to the Father, and to the Son, and to the Holy Spirit, both now and ever, and unto the ages of ages. Amen.

THE MAGNIFICAT, LUKE, CHAPTER 1, VERSES 46-55, TAKEN FROM THE ENGLISH ORTHODOX LITURGY

The Magnificat or Song of Theotokos (God-bearer) is the hymn of praise Mary uttered after being visited by the Angel Gabriel. The choice of a lowly, humble young woman to bear the Son of God, is a reminder that none are too insignificant to receive the grace of the Lord.

"And [Mary] gave birth to her firstborn son and wrapped him in swaddling cloths and laid him in a manger, because there was no place for them in the inn."

LUKE, CHAPTER 2, VERSE 7, ENGLISH STANDARD VERSION

While these simple words are familiar, they contain depths of meaning that continue to astonish. Christ as the *firstborn* shows his dominion and brotherhood with humanity. The *swaddling cloths* prefigure his burial shroud. Most powerfully, the exclusion from the inn and the humble surrounds of the manager powerfully remind us that Christ is humble, and within this humility we are able to meet God.

"The shepherds said one to another, *'Let us now go even unto Bethlehem and see this thing which has come to pass, which the Lord hath made known unto us.'* And they came with haste and found Mary and Joseph, and the Babe lying in a manger."

LUKE, CHAPTER 2, VERSES 15-16, 21ST-CENTURY KING JAMES VERSION

Shepherds, the lowliest of men, were the first people to visit the Christ child. Always cherish this image: that none are too lowly or excluded or marginalized to meet Jesus.

"For God so loved the world, that he gave his only begotten Son, that whosoever believeth in him should not perish, but have everlasting life."

JESUS, SPEAKING IN JOHN, CHAPTER 3, VERSE 16, KING JAMES BIBLE

Christian faith does not exclude the use of human reason. Put your mind to this passage. What does it mean? Is it true? Does it make sense? How does it make you feel? Does it resonate with you? If so, repeat the passage and let it settle within your mind's library of useful words.

HOW TO APPROACH THE BIBLE

EUANGELION	*Euangelion* – good news: from eu – good and *angelion* from *angelos* – messenger
GOSPEL	good news – from *godspel* Old English, good message
EVANGELIST	bringer of good news

Understanding the formation of words helps us to penetrate the meaning of these ancient concepts. Gospels are good messages sent by God's messengers. By receiving and sharing the good news we enter into a venerable chain of divine messaging.

"For whatever was written in former days was written for our instruction, that through endurance and through the encouragement of the scriptures we might have hope."

ROMANS, CHAPTER 15, VERSE 4, ENGLISH STANDARD VERSION

C.S. Lewis coined the term 'chronological snobbery' – that some of us living in the modern world have towards ancient scriptures: it must be wrong because it's old. He encouraged us instead to 'let the breezes of centuries' blow through our minds.

“You who want
knowledge,
seek the Oneness
within.

There you
will find
the clear mirror
already waiting.”

HADEWIJCH,
13TH-CENTURY DUTCH MYSTIC

“Then he opened their minds to understand the scriptures.”

LUKE, CHAPTER 24, VERSE 45

Do not be afraid to read aloud when studying the Bible. Savour each word as if it were a tasty morsel. If the passage is still thick with mystery, read again, aloud or in a slow whisper until the meaning unfolds.

Martin Luther taught the Four Strands technique when approaching Bible reading. When reading a passage ask yourself:

INSTRUCTION What is God teaching me here?

THANKSGIVING For what is God calling me to be thankful?

CONFESSION What is God asking me to admit?

PRAYER What is my response to God?

"Blessed Lord, who caused all holy scriptures to be written for our learning: Grant us so to hear them, read, mark, learn and inwardly digest them, that we may embrace and ever hold fast the blessed hope of everlasting life, which you have given us in our Savior Jesus Christ; who lives and reigns with thee and the Holy Spirit, one God, for ever and ever. Amen."

BOOK OF COMMON PRAYER

"In those days Jesus came from Nazareth of Galilee and was baptized by John in the Jordan. And when he came up out of the water, immediately he saw the heavens being torn open and the Spirit descending on him like a dove."

MARK, CHAPTER 1, VERSES 9–11, ENGLISH STANDARD VERSION

"You are my beloved Son; with you I am well pleased."

MARK, CHAPTER 1, VERSE 11, ENGLISH STANDARD VERSION

GOD SPOKE THESE WORDS AFTER JESUS'S BAPTISM WHEN THE VEIL BETWEEN EARTH AND HEAVEN WAS TORN ASUNDER.

When contemplating your own past, or future baptism, consider carefully the above words from God: *"You are my beloved Son; with you I am well pleased."* Dare we dream that these words could apply also to us? Medieval theologian Thomas Aquinus certainly thought so, believing that through baptism, we all become the adopted children of God.

"The heavens were torn open."

There are passages in the Bible where the heavens are torn open and God reveals himself clearly to humans. Challenge yourself to be alert for such moments: the rays of light between clouds, a sudden explosion of family love, an astonishing act of kindness. These moments of profound clarity and connection are not unique to the Bible but can be experienced in ordinary life today.

MEETING CHRIST

"Jesus began to preach, 'Repent, for the kingdom of heaven has come near.'"

MATTHEW, CHAPTER 4, VERSE 17, NEW INTERNATIONAL VERSION

Understand the message of Christ in its simplest form: *"Repent, for the kingdom of heaven has come near."* Savour the words and consider in your heart what they mean for you:

- A call to abandon a self-centred life
- A call to align with God, not our own selfish desires
- An understanding that through the birth of Jesus, the kingdom of God, has become a present reality
- An appreciation that to *repent*, is not a mere feeling of sorrow for past misdeeds, but a turning of the mind towards God.

"If you remain in me and my words remain in you, ask whatever you wish, and it will be done for you."

JESUS, SPEAKING IN JOHN, CHAPTER 15, VERSE 7, NEW INTERNATIONAL VERSION

"Mercy and truth have met together;
Righteousness and peace have kissed.
Truth shall spring out of the earth,
And righteousness shall look down
from heaven. Yes, the Lord will give
what is good."

PSALM 85, VERSES 10–12, NEW KING JAMES VERSION

If you struggle to pray for yourself, let your thoughts rest on someone who needs help. Use these words as a foundation on which to build prayers for others.

Christ with me,
Christ before me,
Christ behind me,
Christ in me,
Christ beneath me,
Christ above me,
Christ on my right,
Christ on my left,
Christ when I lie down,
Christ when I sit down,
Christ when I arise,
Christ in the heart of every man who thinks of me,
Christ in the mouth of everyone who speaks of me,
Christ in every eye that sees me,
Christ in every ear that hears me.

FROM THE *BREASTPLATE OF SAINT PATRICK*, A 5TH-CENTURY ROMANO-BRITISH SAINT

"Blessed are the poor in spirit,
For theirs is the kingdom of heaven.
Blessed are those who mourn,
For they shall be comforted.
Blessed are the meek,
For they shall inherit the earth.
Blessed are those who hunger
and thirst for righteousness,
For they shall be filled."

JESUS DELIVERING THE SERMON ON THE MOUNT, MATTHEW,
CHAPTER 5, VERSES 3-6, NEW KING JAMES VERSION

"Blessed are the merciful,
For they shall obtain mercy.
Blessed are the pure in heart,
For they shall see God.
Blessed are the peacemakers,
For they shall be called sons of God.
Blessed are those who are
persecuted for righteousness' sake,
For theirs is the kingdom of heaven."

JESUS DELIVERING THE SERMON ON THE MOUNT, MATTHEW,
CHAPTER 5, VERSES 7–10, NEW KING JAMES VERSION

The Beatitudes found in the Sermon on the Mount define true happiness. They are not only gentle consolations for those who suffer, but a radical call for the upturning of what is understood to be vital for spiritual union with God.

Poor, mournful, meek, hungry, merciful, pure, peacemaker, persecuted… how many of these qualities do we have, or lack? Are we able to view the Beatitudes as a divine roadmap that will lead to our soul to union with God through grace-enabled humility?

"But I say to you who hear: Love your enemies, do good to those who hate you, bless those who curse you, and pray for those who spitefully use you."

JESUS SPEAKING DURING HIS SERMON ON THE MOUNT,
LUKE, CHAPTER 6, VERSES 27–28, NEW KING JAMES VERSION

Love your enemies: Is there a more challenging command? How can you love your enemies today?

"And just as you want men to do to you, you also do to them likewise."

JESUS IN LUKE CHAPTER 6, VERSE 31, NEW KING JAMES VERSION

Known as the "golden rule", Jesus commands us to treat others as you would like to be treated. It sounds easy, but is it? Try it today, right this moment.

Turn that which is evil in me into good,
That which is good into better,
My mourning into joy,
My wandering feet into the right path,
My ignorance into knowledge of your truth,
My lukewarmness into zeal,
My fear into love,
All my material good into a spiritual gift,
All my earthly desires into heavenly,
All that is transient into the eternal,
Everything human into the divine.

THOMAS À KEMPIS, GERMAN-DUTCH MYSTIC

O eternal Light, shine into our hearts.
O eternal Goodness, deliver us from evil.
O eternal Power, be our support.
Eternal Wisdom, scatter the darkness
of our ignorance.
Eternal Pity, have mercy upon us.

ALCUIN, CAROLINGIAN SCHOLAR

Remember that these powerful words are not exclusive. They are not reserved for the chosen few, for scholars in ivory towers or the elite: these words are for everyone. Give yourself permission to enter into contemplation of divine mysteries.

O most merciful redeemer, friend and brother, may we know you more clearly, love you more dearly, and follow you more nearly.

RICHARD OF CHICHESTER, ENGLISH SAINT

"Then Jesus spoke to them again, saying, 'I am the light of the world. He who follows Me shall not walk in darkness, but have the light of life.'"

JOHN, CHAPTER 8, VERSE 12, NEW KING JAMES VERSION

Today, mediate, mull over, pray about the promise of *having the light of life*. What does this mean to you? To others? To Christ? Will you accept the gift?

"Jesus came into Galilee, proclaiming the gospel of God, and saying, 'The time is fulfilled, and the kingdom of God is at hand; repent and believe in the gospel.'"

MARK, CHAPTER 1, VERSES 14–15, ENGLISH STANDARD VERSION

If you are a beginner in faith and trying to live in love, let these words of comfort wash over you. Be soothed by their promise of protection and care for your wellbeing.

HOW TO PRAY

If prayer is new to you, or an old habit that has faded away, revive the practice of prayer with the ACTS method:

ADORATION	Acknowledge the wonder of the Lord
CONTRITION	Find the courage to fess up
THANKFULNESS	Remember all that is deserving of gratitude
SUPPLICATION	Share your love by asking the Lord for protection and support for yourself and others

"And when you pray, do not heap up empty phrases as the Gentiles do, for they think that they will be heard for their many words."

MATTHEW, CHAPTER 6, VERSE 7, ENGLISH STANDARD VERSION

When praying, Jesus reminds us not to be mechanical, nor to show off, nor to make an exhibition of ourselves for others. When words or prayers feel challenging, remember this passage.

"In your occupations, try to possess your soul in peace. It is not a good plan to be in haste to perform any action that it may be sooner over. On the contrary, you should accustom yourself to do whatever you have to do with tranquillity, in order that you may retain the possession of yourself and of settled peace."

MADAME GUYON, FRENCH MYSTIC, WHO PURSUED *QUIETISM*: FINDING GOD IN SILENCE, IN LISTENING, AND IN MENTAL AND PHYSICAL STILLNESS.

Today, will you bustle? Today, will you busy yourself unnecessarily? Today, will you slow yourself and take gentle care over each action and interaction?

*"Prayer consists of attention…
It is the orientation of all the attention
of which the soul is capable towards God.
The quality of the attention counts
for much in the quality of prayer."*

SIMONE WEIL, FRENCH MYSTIC

Prayerful attention

If only for a minute, three minutes, five minutes, guide all your attention – *all of it* – to God. Without requesting anything simply let your mind inhabit the idea of God. Let your mind escape from earthly weights and ascend towards the love of God.

"In whatever state a soul may be, it ought to pray. A soul which is pure and beautiful must pray, or else it will lose its beauty; a soul which is striving after this purity must pray, or else it will never attain it; a soul which is newly converted must pray, or else it will fall again; a sinful soul, plunged in sins, must pray so that it might rise again. There is no soul which is not bound to pray, for every single grace comes to the soul through prayer."

SAINTT FAUSTINA, POLISH NUN

When asked how to pray, 4th-century desert father Saint Macarius – who dedicated his life to prayer – said:

"There is no need at all to make long discourse; it is enough to stretch out one's hand, and say, 'Lord as you will, and as you know, have mercy.'"

Are you able to stretch out your hands and ask for mercy today?

After Jesus had been praying, his disciples asked Jesus to teach them how to pray. When we pray the Lord's Prayer, also known as the Pater Nosta (Our Father), we are praying words spoken through the lips of Christ.

"And he said unto them,
'When ye pray, say,
Our Father which art in heaven,
Hallowed be thy name.
Thy kingdom come.
Thy will be done, as in heaven, so in earth.
Give us day by day our daily bread.
And forgive us our sins;
for we also forgive every one that is indebted to us.
And lead us not into temptation;
but deliver us from evil.'"

LUKE, CHAPTER 11, VERSES 1–4, KING JAMES BIBLE

Stop. Be still. Listen.
Immerse yourself in the divine space.

Without words, contemplative prayer allows the person to simply experience the divine presence. Allocate time and find a space, indoors or outdoors where your body and mind are at peace. Be still in the presence of the Lord. Simply allow yourself time to share with the divine. If you fear you will not feel the divine, remember that Jesus dwells in our hearts through faith.

"What is meditating on Christ? It is simply this, thinking habitually and constantly of him and of his deeds and sufferings. It is to have him before our minds as one whom we may contemplate, worship, and address when we rise up, when we lie down, when we eat and drink, when we are at home and abroad, when we are working, or walking, or at rest, when we are alone, and again when we are in company; this is meditating."

JOHN HENRY NEWMAN, CATHOLIC CARDINAL

"Let nothing disturb you, let nothing frighten you, all things are passing away: God never changes. Patience obtains all things. Whoever has God lacks nothing; God alone suffices."

STAINT TERESA OF ÁVILA, SPANISH MYSTIC

It is said that the way to heaven is through prayer. Start small and whisper these words.

God be in my head,
And in my understanding;
God be in my eyes,
And in my looking;
God be in my mouth,
And in my speaking;
God be in my heart,
And in my thinking;
God be at my end,
And at my departing.

FROM THE SARUM PRIMER, A COLLECTION OF PRAYERS USED IN MEDIEVAL SALISBURY

Lord Jesus Christ, son of God,
have mercy on me a sinner.
Lord Jesus Christ, son of God,
have mercy on me a sinner.
Lord Jesus Christ, son of God,
have mercy on me a sinner.

With its origins lying in the ancient eastern deserts, the Jesus Prayer, said as often as needed, has swathed millions of Christians throughout history with a protective armour.

"Rejoice always, pray without ceasing, in everything give thanks; for this is the will of God in Christ Jesus for you."

1 THESSALONIANS, CHAPTER 5, VERSES 16–18, NEW KING JAMES VERSION

Pray without ceasing – it's a tall order.
What does this mean?

- To be in constant communion with Christ
- To not limit prayer to formalized settings
- To not limit yourself in your prayer practice
- A spiritual awareness of the nurturing practice of prayer
- A recognition that our prayers will always be heard

"And I tell you, ask, and it will be given to you; seek, and you will find; knock, and it will be opened to you. For everyone who asks receives, and the one who seeks finds, and to the one who knocks it will be opened."

JESUS DEMONSTRATING THE POWER AND EFFECTIVENESS OF PRAYER, IN LUKE, CHAPTER 11, VERSES 9–10, ENGLISH STANDARD VERSION

"There was a judge who neither feared God nor respected people. And there was a widow in that same town who kept coming to him and pleading for her rights… For a long time the judge refused to act, but at last he said to himself, 'Even though I don't fear God or respect people, yet because of all the trouble this widow is giving me, I will see to it that she gets her rights…'" And the Lord continued, *'Listen to what that corrupt judge said. Now, will God not judge in favour of his own people who cry to him day and night for help? Will he be slow to help them? I tell you, he will judge in their favour and do it quickly.'"*

JESUS TELLING THE PARABLE OF THE 'PERSISTENT WIDOW'
IN LUKE, CHAPTER 18, VERSES 2-8, GOOD NEWS BIBLE

"Now, will God not judge in favour of his own people who cry to him day and night for help? Will he be slow to help them? I tell you, he will judge in their favour and do it quickly."

JESUS TELLING THE PARABLE OF THE 'PERSISTENT WIDOW'
IN LUKE, CHAPTER 18, VERSES 2-8, GOOD NEWS BIBLE

Draw strength from Jesus's promise that God will hear the cries of those who call for help.

"Therefore I tell you, whatever you ask for in prayer, believe that you have received it, and it will be yours."

JESUS SPEAKING IN MARK, CHAPTER 11, VERSE 24, NEW INTERNATIONAL VERSION

Sometimes all we can manage is the contemplation of a few words. Use a single line from scripture as a repeated method of asking God to draw near.

"Your Father knows what you need before you ask him."

JESUS, SPEAKING IN MATTHEW, CHAPTER 6, VERSE 8, NEW STANDARD VERSION

When praying, dare you trust that simply attempting communion with God is sufficient and He will provide what you need without you even asking for help?

"Which one of you, if his son asks him for bread, will give him a stone? Or if he asks for a fish, will give him a serpent? If you then, who are evil, know how to give good gifts to your children, how much more will your Father who is in heaven give good things to those who ask him!"

JESUS SPEAKING IN MATTHEW, CHAPTER 7, VERSES 9–11

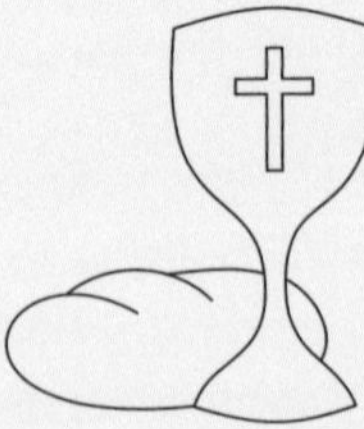

COMMUNING WITH CHRIST

"You are my friends."

JESUS CHRIST TO HIS DISCIPLES, JOHN, CHAPTER 15, VERSE 14,
NEW INTERNATIONAL VERSION

Remember: disciples are those who *learn from*. If we too learn from Jesus, he counts us as his *friends*.

O God let me know you and love you so that I may rejoice in you. And if I cannot know you, love you, rejoice in you fully in this life, let me go forward from day to day, until that knowledge, joy and love at last may be full. Let the knowledge of you grow in me here, and there become full; let the love of you increase in me here and become full; so that my joy may here become great in hope and full in fruition.

SAINT ANSELM, MEDIEVAL THEOLOGIAN

Almighty God, give us the…
Wisdom to perceive you
Intellect to understand you
Diligence to seek you
Patience to wait for you
Vision to behold you
A heart to meditate upon you
A life to proclaim you.

SAINT BENEDICT, FATHER OF MONASTICISM

O let me hear you speaking
in accents clear and still;
above the storms of passion,
the murmurs of self-will:
O speak to reassure me,
to hasten or control;
and speak to make me listen,
O Guardian of my soul.

FROM THE HYMN, *O JESUS I HAVE PROMISED*, BY J.E. BODE

"Is a lamp brought in to be put under a basket, or under a bed, and not on a stand? For nothing is hidden except to be made manifest; nor is anything secret except to come to light. If anyone has ears to hear, let him hear."

JESUS SPEAKING IN MARK, CHAPTER 4, VERSES 21-23, ENGLISH STANDARD VERSION

We are reminded that there are no secrets; the good news that Jesus brings is not to be hidden, but shared.

Lord, I have sought your face; your face Lord, will I seek. Hide not your face from me. Raise me up out of myself towards you. Cleanse, heal, enliven and enlighten the eye of my mind that I may look unto you. Allow my soul to gather its strength once more and with all the power of my understanding, strive after you O Lord.

SAINT ANSELM, MEDIEVAL THEOLOGIAN

Today, contemplate the image of God turning his face towards us. How can you turn your face to shine upon others?

I am not worthy, Lord and master that you should come under the roof of my soul; but since you desire to dwell within me, O lover of humankind, I am bold to draw near.

JOHN CHRYSOSTOM, ARCHBISHOP OF CONSTANTINOPLE

Christian faith does not exclude the use of human reason. Put your mind to this passage. *What does it mean? Is it true? Does it make sense? How does it make you feel? Does it resonate with you?* If so, repeat the passage and let it settle within your mind's library.

"Then he [Jesus] looked at those seated in a circle around him and said, 'Here are my mother and my brothers! Whoever does God's will is my brother and sister and mother.'"

MARK, CHAPTER 3, VERSES 34–35, NEW INTERNATIONAL VERSION

Jesus's message can be difficult to hear: how do we know God's will? How may we follow God's will? God's will feels remote and hard to read or understand. In a bid to become Jesus's brothers and sisters we are wise to remember this commandment, and therefore God's will: *to love one another.*

"Therefore gird up the loins of your mind; be sober and hope to the end for the grace that is to be brought unto you at the revelation of Jesus Christ."

1 PETER, CHAPTER 1, VERSE 13, 21ST-CENTURY KING JAMES VERSION

"Gird up the loins of your mind" is quite the image.

What are the loins of our mind? Our thoughts? Our logical thinking process? Our mental alertness? A preparation of our mind for action? The directing of our intellect to that which will please Jesus?

At its simplest, the message is suggestive of a "gathering" of thoughts in order to go on resolutely, in accordance with Christ's love.

"There are only three types of people: those who have found God and serve him, those who have not found God and seek him, and those who live not seeking, or finding him. The first are rational and happy, the second unhappy and rational, and the third foolish and unhappy."

BLAISE PASCAL, FRENCH PHILOSOPHER

HOSPITALITY

"And you shall say: 'Peace be to my brethren, and to thee, and peace to thy house, and peace to all that thou hast'."

1 SAMUEL, CHAPTER 25, VERSE 6, 21ST-CENTURY KING JAMES VERSION

"Brotherly love must continue. Do not neglect hospitality, because through it some have entertained angels without knowing it. Remember those in prison as though you were in prison with them, and those ill-treated as though you too felt their torment."

HEBREWS 13, VERSES 1-3, NEW ENGLISH TRANSLATION

If you like this passage, share it. Create a picture quote and send to friend. Pin on the refrigerator, next to the bathroom mirror, your laptop screen saver. Words are not lifeless, but they do need to be read, understood, and spoken, to live.

"Our love of neighbour is the measure of our love of God. For Christians – and not only for them – no one is a 'stranger.' The love of Christ knows no borders."

SAINT TERESA BENEDICTA OF THE CROSS, CARMELITE NUN

"Jesus said to the servants, 'Fill the jars with water.' And they filled them up to the brim. And he said to them, 'Now draw some out and take it to the master of the feast.'"

JOHN, CHAPTER 2, VERSES 7–8, ENGLISH STANDARD VERSION

The wedding at Cana where Jesus turned the water into wine, was Jesus's first miracle. There is joy to be found here, a wedding party feasting, eating and drinking. The miracle marks a new joyous covenant (promise) with God, where we will be transformed by the abundant blessings of Christ.

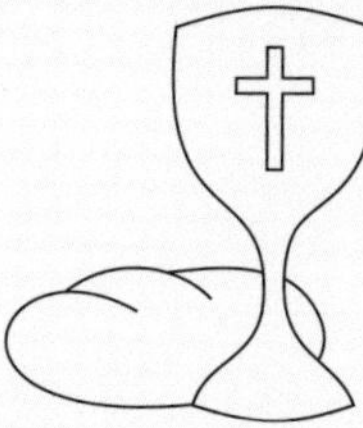

"One of his disciples, Andrew, Simon Peter's brother, said to him, 'There is a boy here who has five barley loaves and two fish, but what are they for so many?' Jesus said, 'Have the people sit down.' Now there was much grass in the place. So the men sat down, about five thousand in number. Jesus then took the loaves, and when he had given thanks, he distributed them to those who were seated. So also the fish, as much as they wanted."

JOHN, CHAPTER 6, VERSES 8–11, ENGLISH STANDARD VERSION

18 MARCH

By feeding the five thousand with a mere five loaves and two fishes, Jesus performed a magnificent miracle, attending to the most basic needs of ordinary humans. Picture those loaves and fish when feeling you don't have enough, be generous with what little you have, and seek to replicate the abundant hospitality of Christ at the feeding of the five thousand.

"From the sky you send rain on the hills,
and the earth is filled with your blessings.
You make grass grow for the cattle
and plants for us to use,
so that we can grow our crops
and produce wine to make us happy,
olive oil to make us cheerful,
and bread to give us strength."

PSALM 104, VERSES 10-15, GOOD NEWS BIBLE

Contemplate the luxury of delicious food and drink shared with friends with this ancient grace.

"While he was having dinner at Matthew's home, many tax collectors and sinners arrived and began eating with Jesus and his disciples. The Pharisees saw this and asked his disciples, 'Why does your teacher eat with tax collectors and sinners?' When Jesus heard that, he said, 'Healthy people don't need a physician, but sick people do.'"

MATTHEW, CHAPTER 9, VERSES 10–12, INTERNATIONAL STANDARD VERSION

How often do any of us dine with sinners and outcasts? How often do any of us show hospitality to those who society despises? Perhaps we are therefore the real sinners and outcasts? How moved would we be to be invited to eat with the Son of God?

Why not plan to share a meal with those on the edges of society, those who are looked down upon, who are shunned as being socially unacceptable.

"She extends her hand to the poor, yes, she reaches out her hands to the needy."

PROVERBS, CHAPTER 31, VERSE 20, NEW KING JAMES VERSION

"When you give a dinner or a supper, do not ask your friends, your brothers, your relatives, nor rich neighbours, lest they also invite you back, and you be repaid. But when you give a feast, invite the poor, the maimed, the lame, the blind. And you will be blessed, because they cannot repay you; for you shall be repaid at the resurrection of the just."

JESUS SPEAKING IN LUKE, CHAPTER 14, VERSES 12–14, NEW KING JAMES VERSION

"There is no beautifier of complexion, or form, or behaviour, like the wish to scatter joy and not pain around us."

RALPH WALDO EMERSON, AMERICAN WRITER

25 MARCH

"If any one forces you to go one mile, go with him two miles. Give to him who begs from you, and do not refuse him who would borrow from you."

JESUS SPEAKING IN MATTHEW, CHAPTER 5, VERSES 41–42, REVISED STANDARD VERSION

"I was hungry and you gave me food,
I was thirsty and you gave me drink,
I was a stranger and you welcomed me,
I was naked and you clothed me,
I was sick and you visited me,
I was in prison and you came to me…
…Truly, I say to you,
As you did it to one of the least of
these my brethren, you did it to me."

JESUS TEACHING IN MATTHEW, CHAPTER 25, VERSES 35–40, REVISED STANDARD EDITION

"If any man desire to be first, the same shall be last of all, and servant of all."

JESUS SPEAKING TO HIS DISCIPLES IN MARK, CHAPTER 9, VERSE 35, KING JAMES BIBLE

LOVE

"This is my commandment, that you love one another as I have loved you."

JESUS SPEAKING IN JOHN, CHAPTER 15, VERSE 12, KING JAMES BIBLE

"This is my commandment, that you love one another as I have loved you."

Believed by many to be the most important passage ever spoken: *love one another as I have loved you*, Jesus changed the world. With these meagre words Jesus directed the human heart towards love. Not power, not glory, not revenge, but love.

"Gather gladness from the skies
Take a lesson from the ground
Flowers do open their heavenward eyes
And a Spring-time joy have found
Earth throws Winter's robes away,
Decks herself for Easter Day."

GERARD MANLEY HOPKINS, POET AND PRIEST

Breathing exercise

Close your eyes and open your heart to Christ. Breathe in slowly and picture love. Breathe out slowly and picture fear. Breathe in love, breathe out fear, until you feel your heart infused with perfect love.

Ubi caritas et amor,
Deus ibi est.

Where there is charity and love, there is God.

Known as the *Ubi caritas*, this is a Gregorian chant that has been sung since the 4th century. It translates into English as, *Where there is charity and love, there is God.* If possible, seek out a recording of *Ubi caritas* and let this divine chant always remind you, that *where there is love, there is God.*

A lawyer asks Jesus a question about which of the commandments is the greatest, Jesus replies:

"You shall 'Love the Lord your God with all your heart and with all your soul and with all your mind and with all your strength.' The second is this: 'Love your neighbour as yourself.' There is no other commandment greater than these."

MARK, CHAPTER 12, VERSE 30–31, NEW INTERNATIONAL VERSION

"There is no other commandment greater than these."

Besides from attending church, praying every day and doing good works, are you following Jesus's most important commandments: to love God and love your neighbour?

"Do good under all circumstances, but with no care for any profit, or any blessedness, or any damnation, or any salvation, or any martyrdom; but all you do or omit should be for the honour of love."

HADEWIJCH, DUTCH MYSTIC

If you are a beginner in faith and trying to live in love, let these words of comfort wash over you. Be soothed by their promise of protection and care for your wellbeing.

"As the Father has loved me, so have I loved you. Now remain in my love. If you keep my commands, you will remain in my love, just as I have kept my Father's commands and remain in his love. I have told you this so that my joy may be in you and that your joy may be complete."

JESUS SPEAKING IN JOHN 15, VERSES 9–11, NEW INTERNATIONAL VERSION

Tolstoy wrote about what it means to love your neighbour.

"Not someone agreeable or useful, but all men equally, though they are the most disagreeable and hostile men. Only he can love his neighbour in this manner who loves God, that God who is the same in all men."

LEO TOLSTOY, FROM *THE WAY OF LIFE*

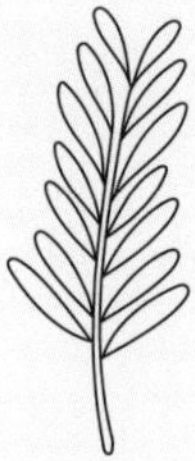

"Until I see that the principal precept of Christ, to love your enemy, is observed, I shall not believe that those who call themselves Christians are Christians indeed."

GOTTHOLD LESSING, GERMAN PHILOSOPHER

Do you love your enemy?
Do you pray for your enemy?
How do you love your enemy?
How do you pray for your enemy?

"Love is patient and kind; love does not envy or boast; it is not arrogant or rude. It does not insist on its own way; it is not irritable or resentful; it does not rejoice at wrongdoing, but rejoices with the truth. Love bears all things, believes all things, hopes all things, endures all things. Love never ends."

SAINT PAUL, 1 CORINTHIANS, CHAPTER 13, VERSES 4–8, ENGLISH STANDARD VERSION

Daily love checklist:

Are you patient and kind?
Do you envy others and boast?
Are you arrogant and rude?
Do you insist on your own way?
Are you irritable and resentful?
Do you rejoice at wrongdoing?

TRAVEL

"Behold I am with you, and will keep you wherever you go."

GENESIS, CHAPTER 28, VERSE 15, ENGLISH STANDARD VERSION

"Remember, I will be with you and protect you wherever you go."

GENESIS, CHAPTER 28, VERSE 15, GOOD NEWS BIBLE

"Now pay attention! I'm here with you, and I'm going to be watching over you wherever you go."

GENESIS, CHAPTER 28, VERSE 15, INTERNATIONAL STANDARD VERSION

Whatever translation you prefer, the message is the same: God's presence is constant.

"But one thing I do: Forgetting what is behind and straining towards what is ahead, I press on towards the goal to win the prize for which God has called me heavenward in Christ Jesus."

SAINT PAUL, PHILIPPIANS, CHAPTER 3, VERSES 13–14

With eyes on the prize of ever closeness to God, Saint Paul encourages us keep the momentum going. By reaching forward and upwards, we may continue in our lifelong journey towards closer resemble to the example of Christ.

JOY IN ART AND MUSIC

"Music, 'the sacred sound through which all creation resounds.'"

HILDEGARD VON BINGEN, GERMAN AND NUN AND MEDIEVAL COMPOSER OF THE 'SYMPHONY OF THE HARMONY OF CELESTIAL REVELATIONS'

When seeking peace, use harmonious music to assist in your connection with the divine. By mirroring the angelic harmonies of the heavens, it is possible to tune into another way of being.

"The perfections of God are those of our souls, but he possesses them in boundless measure; he is an ocean; to us only drops have been granted; there is in us some power, some knowledge, some goodness, but in God they are all in their entirety. Order, proportions, harmony delight us; painting and music are samples of these: God is all order; he always keeps truth of proportions, he makes universal harmony; all beauty is an effusion of his rays."

GOTTFRIED LEIBNITZ, GERMAN PHILOSOPHER

"But the Holy Spirit produces this kind of fruit in our lives: love, joy, peace, patience, kindness, goodness, faithfulness, gentleness, and self-control. There is no law against these things!"

SAINT PAUL, ADDRESSING THE GALATIANS, CHAPTER 5, VERSES 22–23, NEW LIVING BIBLE

"The Lord bless you and keep you;
The Lord make his face shine on you
And be gracious to you;
The Lord turn his face towards you
And give you peace."

NUMBERS, CHAPTER 6, VERSES 24–26, NEW INTERNATIONAL VERSION

Remember that these powerful words are not exclusive. They are not reserved for the chosen few, for scholars in ivory towers or the elite: these words are for everyone. Give yourself permission to enter into contemplation of divine mysteries.

Art symbolizes heaven,
but Love is God
And makes heaven.

FROM *AURORA LEIGH* BY ELIZABETH BARRATT BROWNING

"Do not think it wasted time to submit yourself to any influence which may bring upon you any noble feeling."

JOHN RUSKIN, ARTIST AND WRITER

Establish what ravishing beauty, activity or experience enhances an internal noble feeling. Do more of it.

20 APRIL

"Help us to recognize your voice,
Help us not to be allured by the madness of the world,
So that we may never fall away from you,
O Lord Jesus Christ."

ALBRECH DÜRER, ARTIST

NATURE

"Then God said, 'Let the waters abound with an abundance of living creatures, and let birds fly above the earth across the face of the firmament of the heavens.' So God created great sea creatures and every living thing that moves, with which the waters abounded, according to their kind, and every winged bird according to its kind. And God saw that it was good. And God blessed them, saying, 'Be fruitful and multiply, and fill the waters in the seas, and let birds multiply on the earth.'"

GENESIS, CHAPTER 1, VERSES 20–22, NEW KING JAMES VERSION

Today what can we do to cherish the abundance of living creatures that God has created?

"Consider the lilies, how they grow: they toil not, neither do they spin; yet I say unto you, even Solomon in all his glory was not arrayed like one of these. But if God doth so clothe the grass in the field, which today is, and tomorrow is cast into the oven; how much more shall he clothe you, O ye of little faith? And seek not ye what ye shall eat, and what ye shall drink, neither be ye of doubtful mind."

JESUS SPEAKING IN LUKE, CHAPTER 12, VERSES 27–29, ENGLISH REVISED VERSION

Discover the concept of *viriditas*, the greening power of nature. Viriditas was explored by medieval composer Hildegard von Bingen. She used her music to connect the pulsing green life of nature with the fresh reviving life of the divine. Experience the divine in groves, in parklands, in the unfurling coils of spring.

O noblest green viridity,
you're rooted in the sun
and in the clear,
bright calm
you shine within a wheel
no earthly excellence
can comprehend:

You are surrounded by
the embraces of the service,
the ministries divine.
As morning's dawn you blush,
as sunny flame you burn.

HILDEGARD VON BINGEN, GERMAN NUN

"Nature is God's living, visible garment."

JOHANN WOLFGANG VON GOETHE, GERMAN WRITER

"Let the heavens rejoice, and let the earth be glad, let the sea be moved, and the fulness thereof.

The fields and all things that are in them shall be joyful. Then shall all the trees of the woods rejoice."

PSALM 96, VERSES 11–12, KING JAMES BIBLE

Go outside. Listen to the whisper of God as he speaks through the trees and sings through the sea.

"Let every creature have your love. Love, with its fruits of meekness, patience and humility, is all that we can wish for to ourselves, and our fellow-creatures; for this is to live in God, united to him, both for time and eternity."

WILLIAM LAW, ENGLISH PRIEST

"In his hand is the life of every creature and the breath of all mankind."

JOB, CHAPTER 12, VERSE 10, NEW INTERNATIONAL VERSION

"Nature is too thin a screen,
the glory of the omnipresent
God bursts through everywhere."

RALPH WALDO EMERSON, AMERICAN WRITER

"A heavenly master governs all the world as sovereign of the universe. We are astonished at him by reason of his perfection, we honour him and fall down before him because of his unlimited power. From blind physical necessity, which is always and everywhere the same, no variety adhering to time and place could evolve, and all variety of created objects which represent order and life in the universe could happen only by the wilful reasoning of its original creator, Whom I call the Lord God."

SIR ISAAC NEWTON, IN *PHILOSOPHIAE NATURALIS PRINCIPIA MATHEMATICA*
WHERE HE DEVELOPED LAWS OF GRAVITY

"Everybody needs beauty as well as bread, places to play in and pray in, where nature may heal and give strength to body and soul."

JOHN MUIR, AMERICAN NATURALIST

Feed your soul by connecting, enjoying, feeling vigorously alive, or quietly contemplative, in the rich abundance of nature.

"The poor man had nothing except one little ewe lamb he had bought. He raised it, and it grew up with him and his children. It shared his food, drank from his cup and even slept in his arms. It was like a daughter to him."

2 SAMUEL, CHAPTER 12, VERSE 3, NEW INTERNATIONAL VERSION

Cherish the tenderness of this passage for it teaches us how to care for God's creatures.

3 MAY

"Earth's crammed with heaven, And every common bush afire with God."

FROM *AURORA LEIGH* BY ELIZABETH BARRATT BROWNING

"Everything is part
of one stupendous whole,
Whose body nature is,
and God the soul."

ALEXANDER POPE, ENGLISH POET

"God moves in a mysterious way
His wonders to perform;
He plants His footsteps in the sea
And rides upon the storm."

WILLIAM COWPER, ENGLISH POET

"All that is sweet, delightful, and amiable in this world, in the serenity of the air, the fineness of seasons, the joy of light, the melody of sounds, the beauty of colours, the fragrancy of smells, the splendour of precious stones, is nothing else but heaven breaking through the veil of this world."

WILLIAM LAW, ENGLISH PRIEST

"O woman, what a splendid being you are! For you have set your foundation in the sun, and have conquered the world."

HILDEGARD VON BINGEN, GERMAN NUN

Cherish this observation:
O woman, what a splendid being you are!

"The woman's soul is fashioned as a shelter in which other souls may unfold."

SAINT TERESA BENEDICTA OF THE CROSS, CARMELITE NUN

BATTLE

"In all these things we are more than conquerors through him who loved us. For I am convinced that neither death nor life, neither angels nor demons, neither the present nor the future, nor any powers, neither height nor depth, nor anything else in all creation, will be able to separate us from the love of God that is in Christ Jesus our Lord."

SAINT PAUL, WRITING TO THE ROMANS, CHAPTER 8, VERSES 37–39,
NEW INTERNATIONAL VERSION

"We are more than conquerors."

SAINT PAUL, ROMANS, CHAPTER 8, VERSE 37, NEW INTERNATIONAL VERSION

WRITING TO THE WARRIOR NATION, THE ROMANS, SAINT PAUL WAS ELEGANTLY DEMONSTRATING THAT THE LOVE OF CHRIST IS SO MUCH MORE THAN MERE EARTHLY VICTORY

Are you able to imagine being more than a conqueror? Who is being conquered? What is being conquered?

"For a Christian to be a conqueror is a great thing: how can he be more than a conqueror? … Now this is being more than a conqueror, when weakness overcomes strength, when brute force is baffled by gentleness and love. This is victory indeed, when the little things overcome the great things; when the base things of this world overthrow the mighty; and the things that are not bring to nought the things that are: yet this is just the triumph of grace."

CHARLES SPURGEON, AMERICAN PREACHER

*"Be joyful in hope,
patient in affliction,
faithful in prayer."*

SAINT PAUL, ROMANS, CHAPTER 12,
VERSE 12, NEW INTERNATIONAL VERSION

"Be Lord…
Within me to strengthen me,
Outside me to preserve,
Over me to shelter,
Beneath me to support,
Before me to direct,
Behind me to bring back,
All around to strengthen."

LANCELOT ANDREWES, 17TH-CENTURY TRANSLATOR OF THE KING JAMES BIBLE

"Stand therefore, having fastened on the belt of truth, and having put on the breastplate of righteousness, and, as shoes for your feet, having put on the readiness given by the gospel of peace."

SAINT PAUL, IN EPHESIANS, CHAPTER 6, VERSES 14–15, ENGLISH STANDARD VERSION

"No coward soul is mine,
No trembler in the world's
storm-troubled sphere:
I see Heaven's glories shine,
And faith shines equal,
arming me from fear."

EMILY BRONTË, AUTHOR OF WUTHERING HEIGHTS

"Blessed Lord, you know that I am suspected and despised in many places because of my love for you. Lord, in your mercy, turn all this shame into glory, and give me strength to endure whatever you want me to suffer for love of you."

MEDIEVAL MYSTIC MARGERY KEMPE WAS ARRESTED IN 1417 FOR DEFYING STRICT CHURCH RESTRICTIONS ON WOMEN PREACHERS. THIS IS HER PRAYER FOR DELIVERANCE FROM OPPRESSION. HER WORDS ARE AN ETERNAL PLEA FOR FREEDOM FROM TYRANNY AND THE STRENGTH TO ENDURE IT.

"Do you never get into this state in which your mind is distracted, you know not what to do; you cannot calm and steady yourself ... You will come out of this all right enough. You will be more than a conqueror over mental distress. You will take this burden as well as every other to your Lord, and cast it upon him; and the Holy Ghost, whose office it is to be the Comforter, will say to the troubled waves of your heart, *'Be still.'* Jesus shall say, as he walks the tempest of your soul, *'It is I, be not afraid.'*"

CHARLES SPURGEON, AMERICAN PREACHER

PEACE

"We have peace with God through our Lord Jesus Christ. Through him we have obtained access to this grace in which we stand, and we rejoice in our hope of sharing the glory of God."

SAINT PAUL, FROM ROMANS, CHAPTER 5, VERSES 1–2, REVISED STANDARD VERSION

"O blessed Jesus, give me
stillness of soul in you.
Let your mighty calmness reign in me.
Rule me, O king of gentleness,
king of peace."

SAINT JOHN OF THE CROSS, SPANISH MYSTIC

"God will speak peace into your soul; God will set you on the way; God will bear you above things of sense and praise of people, and things which perish in your grasp, and give you, if even far off, some glimpse of his own, unfading, unsetting, unperishing brightness and bliss and love."

E.B. PUSEY, ENGLISH THEOLOGIAN

Today, try to remember this:
God will speak peace into your soul.

"Make peace with God
and stop treating him like an enemy;
If you do, then he will bless you.
Accept the teaching he gives;
keep his words in your heart."

JOB, CHAPTER 22, VERSES 21–22, GOOD NEWS BIBLE

"God is a tranquil Being and lives in a tranquil eternity. So must your spirit become a tranquil and clear little pool, where the serene light of God can be mirrored. Therefore avoid all that is disquieting and distracting, both within and without. Nothing in the whole world is worth the loss of your peace; even the faults which you have committed should only humble but not disquiet you. Endeavour instead to obtain a continually joyful and peaceful spirit."

"Avoid all anxious care, vexation, murmuring, and melancholy, which darken your soul, and make you unfit for the friendship of God. If you do perceive such feelings arise, turn gently away from them."

GERHARD TERSTEEGEN, GERMAN HYMNIST

"In peace I will both lie down and sleep; for you alone, O Lord, make me dwell in safety."

PSALM 4, VERSE 8, ENGLISH STANDARD VERSION

"I no longer fear God,
but I love him.
For love casts out fear."

SAINT ANTHONY, EGYPTIAN HERMIT

"O Lord who is eternal peace and who gives peace to those who are steadfast in their heart, let your peace be on your servants, that in doing your will, we may ourselves find peace, and bring peace to others, through Jesus Christ our Lord."

FREDERICK B. MACNUTT, WORLD WAR ONE CHAPLAIN WHO CONDUCTED SERVICES ON THE WESTERN FRONT.

"Go forth into the world in peace;
be of good courage;
hold fast that which is good;
render to no one evil for evil;
strengthen the fainthearted;
support the weak;
help the afflicted;
honour all people;
love and serve the Lord,
rejoicing in the power of the Holy Spirit."

BOOK OF COMMON PRAYER

Lord, make me an instrument of your peace,
Where there is hatred, let me sow love,
Where there is injury, pardon;
Where there is doubt, faith;
Where there is despair, hope;
Where there is darkness, light;
Where there is sadness, joy.

SAINT FRANCIS OF ASSISI

"Go and sin no more."

JESUS, JOHN, CHAPTER 8, VERSE 11

These were the words uttered by Jesus after he stopped the stoning of a woman for adultery. *Go and sin no more*. What meaning could this have for you today, tomorrow and beyond?

O divine Master,
grant that I may not so much seek,
To be consoled as to console,
To be understood as to understand,
To be loved as to love.
For it is in giving that we receive,
It is in pardoning that we are pardoned,
And it is in dying that we are born
to eternal life.

SAINT FRANCIS OF ASSISI

SIN

It's a sharp word, "sin", and one that is generally shunned today. To accuse someone of *sinning*, is the ultimate contemporary sin of judgement. And yet, we all know instinctively what a sin is. We know when we have committed one, and when one is committed against us. It stings to the soul.

The word sin is derived from Old English *synn*, *syn* and means "violation of divine law, offense against God; moral wrongdoing," also "injury, mischief; enmity, feud; guilt, crime, misdeed". It is also described as 'falling short or "lawlessness".

If the word frightens, appalls or worries you try to explore why that may be.

"But you know that he appeared so that he might take away our sins. And in him is no sin. No one who lives in him keeps on sinning. No one who continues to sin has either seen him or known him."

1 JOHN, CHAPTER 3, VERSE 5, NEW INTERNATIONAL VERSION

"Hurt not your conscience with any known sin."

SAMUEL RUTHERFORD, SCOTTISH MINISTER

It bears remembering that when sins, small or large, are committed it is the sinner who often suffers the most.

"If you have sinned, do not lie down without repentance; for the want of repentance after one has sinned makes the heart even harder and harder."

JOHN BUNYAN, AUTHOR OF *PILGRIM'S PROGRESS*

"Men never do evil so completely and cheerfully as when they do it from religious conviction."

BLAISE PASCAL, FRENCH PHILOSOPHER

Is there anything worse than a sanctimonious scold? Guard against using your faith or conviction to condemn or oppress others. Remember always that God is love.

"Do not let the sun go down on your anger."

EPHESIANS, CHAPTER 4, VERSE 26, ENGLISH STANDARD VERSION

"Blessed are the merciful, for they shall obtain mercy."

MATTHEW, CHAPTER 5, VERSE 7, 21ST-CENTURY KING JAMES VERSION

In seeking mercy from Jesus, are we able to extend mercy to those who have hurt us or those we love?

"Some Christians have imagined that they could be devout without loving their neighbour, and pious without loving God; or else people have thought that they could love their neighbour without serving him and could love God without knowing him."

GOTTFRIED LEIBNITZ, GERMAN PHILOSOPHER

Today: how may I serve my neighbour and better incline my heart to God?

"You have heard that people were told in the past, 'Do not commit murder; anyone who does will be brought to trial.' But now I tell you: if you are angry with your brother, you will be brought to trial."

MATTHEW, CHAPTER 5, VERSES 21–22, GOOD NEWS BIBLE

What we feel inside influences our actions. We are encouraged to monitor our thoughts, just as carefully as our actions. Try this prayer practice to expel angry thoughts:

Take the *breath of the spirit*. Breath in and on the exhale pray, *"Lord give me your peace."*

"We demolish arguments and every pretension that sets itself up against the knowledge of God, and we take captive every thought to make it obedient to Christ."

2 CORINTHIANS, CHAPTER 10, VERSE 5, NEW INTERNATIONAL VERSION

Read and repeat until you can hear the voice of the divine in your heart.

"We take captive every thought..."

What a powerful action Saint Paul speaks to the Corinthians about. Having the ability to interrupt corrosive and unhelpful thoughts can be transformative. Take captive harmful thoughts and redirect them towards loving kindness.

"My dear brothers and sisters, take note of this: Everyone should be quick to listen, slow to speak and slow to become angry, because human anger does not produce the righteousness that God desires."

1 JAMES, CHAPTER 1, VERSES 19–20, NEW INTERNATIONAL VERSION

Remember...
Quick to listen
Slow to speak
Slow to become angry

"Two things fill the mind with ever new and increasing admiration and awe, the oftener and more steadily we reflect on them: the starry heavens above me and the moral law within me."

IMMANUEL KANT, GERMAN PHILOSOPHER

Are you in touch with your inner moral law?
Does your conscience speak to you?
What does it say?

"Hold fast that which is good."

1 THESSALONIANS, CHAPTER 5, VERSE 21, KING JAMES BIBLE

If you like this passage, share it. Create a picture quote and send to friend. Pin on the refrigerator, next to the bathroom mirror, your laptop screen saver. Words are not lifeless, but they do need to be read, understood, and spoken, to live.

13 JUNE

FORGIVENESS

"Watch yourselves! If your brother sins, rebuke him, and if he repents, forgive him. Even if he sins against you seven times in a day and comes back to you seven times and says, 'I repent,' you must forgive him."

JESUS SPEAKING IN LUKE, CHAPTER 17, VERSE 3, INTERNATIONAL STANDARD VERSION

"Lord Jesus Christ, very sun of the world, ever arising and never going down; whose being gives health and gladness, creates, preserves, and nourishes all things in heaven and in earth. Graciously enlighten my spirit, so the night of sin and the mists of error may be driven away by your inward shining; so that I may go all my life long without stumbling."

ERASMUS, DUTCH THEOLOGIAN

Hold onto the image of *'the mists of error'*. Within Christianity, repentance and forgiveness, errors, like *mist*, dissipate.

"Do not judge, and you will not be judged. Do not condemn, and you will not be condemned. Forgive, and you will be forgiven. Give, and it will be given to you. A good measure, pressed down, shaken together, and running over, will be poured into your lap. The measure that you use for others will be used to measure you."

JESUS SPEAKING IN LUKE, CHAPTER 6, VERSES 37–38, NEW CATHOLIC BIBLE

"Forgive others and God will forgive you."

"Forgive others and God will forgive you."

"Forgive others and God will forgive you."

A prayerful action: absorb this message of forgiveness and act on it. Forgive those who have wronged you; bear them no anger; enjoy the miracle of emotional and spiritual freedom that forgiveness brings.

I offer up unto you my prayers for those especially who have in any matter hurt, grieved, or found fault with me, or who have done me any damage or displeasure.

For all those also whom, at any time, I may have vexed, troubled, burdened, and scandalized, by words or deeds, knowingly or in ignorance; that you will grant us all equally pardon for our offences against each other.

THOMAS À KEMPIS, MEDIEVAL MYSTIC

There is a divine balance here; when we forgive others, we too are forgiven.

When Peter the disciple asked how many times he should forgive someone, Jesus replied:

"I tell you, not just seven times, but 77 times!"

MATTHEW, CHAPTER 18, VERSE 21, INTERNATIONAL STANDARD VERSION

"Then Jesus Christ comes to tell men that they have no other enemies but themselves; that it is their passions which keep them apart from God; that He comes to destroy these, and give them His grace, so as to make of them all one Holy Church."

BLAISE PASCAL, FRENCH PHILOSOPHER

"We experience good only by doing it."

SIMONE WEIL, FRENCH PHILOSOPHER

If we want mercy: practice mercy.
If we want forgiveness: practice forgiveness.
If we want to feel good: do good.

This idea is known today as agentic living – living with agency. We are not the helpless victims of events or the will of others. Instead, by practicing ourselves what we long for, we can shape our lives for the better.

"God's mercy sometimes touches the sinner at the last moment in a wondrous and mysterious way. Outwardly, it seems as if everything were lost, but it is not so. The soul, illumined by a ray of God's powerful final grace, turns to God in the last moment with such a power of love that, in an instant, it receives from God forgiveness of sin and punishment."

SAINT FAUSTINA, 20TH-CENTURY POLISH NUN

"But the tax collector stood at a distance. He would not even look up to heaven, but beat his breast and said, 'God, have mercy on me, a sinner.'"

Jesus promised that this man, humbly repenting of his sins, *'went home justified before God. For all those who exalt themselves will be humbled, and those who humble themselves will be exalted.'"*

LUKE, CHAPTER 18, VERSES 13–14, NEW INTERNATIONAL VERSION

"What we call conscience is the voice of divine love in the deep of our being desiring union with our will; and which by attracting the affections inward, invites them to enter into the harmonious contentment, and fulness of joy which attends the being joined by one spirit to the Lord."

JOHN PIERRPONT GREAVES, ENGLISH MYSTIC

If you find it difficult to articulate a request for forgiveness, try using the words from the *Book of Common Prayer*:

Lord God,
we have sinned against you;
we have done evil in your sight.
We are sorry and repent.
Have mercy on us according to your love.
Wash away our wrongdoing and cleanse
us from our sin.
Renew a right spirit within us
and restore us to the joy of your salvation,
through Jesus Christ our Lord.

"Brothers, sisters, let us remember this: the Lord comes to us when we step back from our presumptuous ego. He can bridge the distance whenever, with honesty and sincerity, we bring our weaknesses before him."

POPE FRANCIS

"We plead with you on Christ's behalf, 'Be reconciled to God!' God made the one who did not know sin to be sin for us, so that in him we would become the righteousness of God."

2 CORINTHIANS, CHAPTER 5 VERSES, 20–21, NEW ENGLISH TRANSLATION

This exquisite passage rests at the heart of the Christian message. Christ has *already* taken on our errors. Our own pain soars from our broken heart to Christ's body on the cross. With this great act of love, we can reconcile with God.

"The Son of Man did not come to be served, but to serve and to give his life as a ransom for many people."

JESUS SPEAKING IN MARK, CHAPTER 10, VERSE 45, INTERNATIONAL STANDARD VERSION

"To say that God turns away from the sinful is like saying that the sun hides from the blind."

SAINT ANTHONY, EGYPTIAN HERMIT

"And when you stand praying, if you hold anything against anyone, forgive them, so that your Father in heaven may forgive you your sins."

JESUS, SPEAKING IN MARK, CHAPTER 11, VERSE 25, NEW INTERNATIONAL VERSION

Lord our God, great, eternal, wonderful in glory, who keeps promises for those who love you with their whole heart, who is the *life* of all, the *help* of those who flee to you, the *hope* of those who cry to you. Cleanse us from our sins, secret and open; and from every thought displeasing to your goodness, – cleanse our bodies and souls, our hearts and consciences, so with a pure heart, and a clear soul, with perfect love and calm hope, we may venture confidently and fearlessly to pray to you.

COPTIC LITURGY OF SAINT BASIL

TRYING TO CHANGE

“Anyone who belongs to Christ is a new person. The past is forgotten, and everything is new.”

2 CORINTHIANS, CHAPTER 5, VERSE 17, CONTEMPORARY ENGLISH VERSION

"Would you like to enjoy life?
Do you want long life and happiness?
Then keep from speaking evil
and from telling lies.
Turn away from evil and do good;
strive for peace with all your heart."

PSALM 34, VERSES 12–14, GOOD NEWS BIBLE

O God, grant that looking upon the face of the Lord as into a glass, we may be changed into His likeness, from glory to glory. Take out of us all pride and vanity, boasting and forwardness; and give us the true courage which shows itself by gentleness; the true wisdom which shows itself by simplicity; and the true power which shows its by modesty.

CHARLES KINGSLEY, SOCIAL REFORMER

Consider which aspects of yourself you would like elevate or soften. How can this be attempted today?

"Do not be yoked together with those who do not believe. For what partnership is there between righteousness and lawlessness? Or what fellowship does light have with darkness?"

2 CORINTHIANS, CHAPTER 6, VERSE 14, CHRISTIAN STANDARD BIBLE

The important word here is *yoked*... this passage is not a message to avoid non-believers. Instead, it is a reminder not to chain yourselves to those who do not walk with Christ.

"Remember… By little and little the mulberry leaf becomes satin. No one can understand prior to experience, the amazing power of small efforts constantly and steadily repeated."

MARY ANNE KELTY, NOVELIST

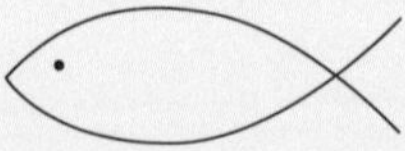

"The bitterest tears shed over graves are for words left unsaid and deeds left undone."

HARRIET BEECHER STOWE, AMERICAN AUTHOR

Do it today: apologize, say sorry, make that call, lavish love on those you love, tie up loose ends. Straight away. Don't delay. That which nags, that which needs to be done, amended and made right, do it right now. This very day.

"Do nothing from selfish ambition or conceit, but in humility count others more significant than yourselves. Let each of you look not only to his own interests, but also to the interests of others."

SAINT PAUL, IN HIS LETTER TO THE PHILIPPIANS, CHAPTER 2, VERSES 3-4, ENGLISH STANDARD VERSION

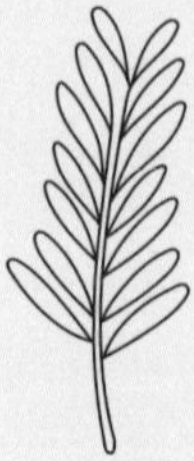

Have we thought irreverently of you O Lord, have we disobeyed your commandments, have we neglected any known duty, or willingly given pain to any human being? Incline us to ask our hearts these questions oh! God, and save us from deceiving ourselves by pride or vanity.

JANE AUSTEN, FROM *ON EACH RETURN OF THE NIGHT*

"Christ has no body but yours,
No hands, no feet on earth but yours,
Yours are the eyes with which He looks
compassion on this world,
Yours are the feet with which He walks to do good,
Yours are the hands, with which He blesses all the world.
Yours are the hands, yours are the feet,
Yours are the eyes, you are His body.
Christ has no body now but yours,
No hands, no feet on earth but yours,
Yours are the eyes with which he looks
compassion on this world.
Christ has no body now on earth but yours."

SAINT TERESA OF ÁVILA, SPANISH NUN

FEELING LOW AND ANXIOUS

"Therefore I tell you, do not be anxious about your life, what you will eat, nor about your body, what you will put on. For life is more than food, and the body more than clothing."

JESUS SPEAKING TO HIS DISCIPLES IN LUKE, CHAPTER 12, VERSES 22–23, ENGLISH STANDARD VERSION

"When I see the blindness and the wretchedness of man, when I regard the whole silent universe, and man without light, left to himself, and, as it were, lost in this corner of the universe, without knowing who has put him there, what he has come to do, what will become of him at death, and incapable of all knowledge, I become terrified, like a man who should be carried in his sleep to a dreadful desert island, and should awake without knowing where he is, and without means of escape."

BLAISE PASCAL, FRENCH PHILOSOPHER

Terror at the emptiness of the universe, and of our own heart without God, is a fear that has gripped people since the dawn of time. When overcome with what seems to be the silence of space, draw strength from the other great Christian thinkers who are honest enough to recognize the abyss.

We are entreated repeatedly in the Bible *not to fear*. Phrases and translations vary but the sentiment expressed hundreds of times, is always the same: *Do not fear, for I am with you.*

"So do not fear, for I am with you; do not be dismayed, for I am your God. I will strengthen you and help you; I will uphold you with my righteous right hand."

ISAIAH CHAPTER 41, VERSE 10.

"Nothing so demoralizes the forces of the soul as fear. Only as we realize the presence of the Lord does fear give place to faith."

SARAH FRANCES SMILEY, AMERICAN QUAKER

There is a compelling idea that there are 365 'fear nots' in the Bible. Though not quite true, there are hundreds of calls to let fear pass by and to trust in the Lord. When fear takes the place of love, we must turn again to the Lord and remember, *be not afraid*.

"I sought the Lord and he answered me, and delivered me from all my fears."

PSALM 34, VERSE 4, ENGLISH REVISED VERSION

"The Lord is my light and my salvation;
Whom shall I fear?
The Lord is the stronghold of my life;
Of whom shall I be afraid?"

PSALM 27, VERSE 1

"And behold, there was a woman who had had a disabling spirit for eighteen years. She was bent over and could not fully straighten herself. When Jesus saw her, he called her over and said to her, 'Woman, you are freed from your disability.' And he laid his hands on her, and immediately she was made straight, and she glorified God."

LUKE, CHAPTER 13, VERSES 11–13, ENGLISH STANDARD VERSION

Imagine having a *disabling spirit* for 18 years; the image is frightening. With this miracle we can picture ourselves. Has our spirit been disabled? Have we been figuratively stooped and crushed for decades? Take heart and remember that Jesus heals.

"My God in whom are all the spring
Of boundless love and grace unknown,
Hide me beneath your spreading wings,
Till the dark cloud is overblown."

ISAAC WATTS, ENGLISH THEOLOGIAN

"And which of you by being anxious can add a single hour to his span of life? If then you are not able to do as small a thing as that, why are you anxious about the rest?"

JESUS SPEAKING TO HIS DISCIPLES, LUKE, CHAPTER 12, VERSES 25–26, ENGLISH STANDARD VERSION

"Be anxious for nothing, but in everything by prayer and supplication, with thanksgiving, let your requests be made known to God."

LETTER OF SAINT PAUL, TO THE PHILIPPIANS, CHAPTER 4, VERSES 6-7, NEW KING JAMES VERSION

Today, remember particularly:
Be anxious for nothing.

God of our life, there are days when the burdens we carry chafe our shoulders and weigh us down; when the road seems dreary and endless, the skies gray and threatening; when our lives have no music in them, and our hearts are lonely, and our souls have lost their courage.

Flood the path with light, run our eyes to where the skies are full of promise; tune our hearts to brave music; give us the sense of comradeship with heroes and saints of every age; and so quicken our spirits that we may be able to encourage the souls of all who journey with us on the road of life, to your honour and glory.

SAINT AUGUSTINE, 4TH-CENTURY CHURCH FATHER

"When Jesus heard it, he saith unto them, 'They that are whole have no need of the physician, but they that are sick: I came not to call the righteous, but sinners to repentance.'"

MARK, CHAPTER TWO, VERSE 17, KING JAMES BIBLE

I came not to call the righteous, but sinners – no matter how wretched you feel, nor how dreadful you perceive your deeds to be, Jesus came to save those who have made mistakes, those in need of help. *I came not to call the righteous, but sinners.*

"After sunset all who had friends who were sick with various diseases brought them to Jesus; he placed his hands on every one of them and healed them all."

LUKE, CHAPTER 4, VERSE 40, GOOD NEWS BIBLE

Jesus, *"healed them all."*

Jesus, *"healed them all."*

Jesus, *"healed them all."*

Not some, not a few, not his favourites, not those who paid, not the elite. Jesus, *"healed them all"*. Remember this: Jesus can heal all of us.

"Jesus left the synagogue and went to Simon's home. Simon's mother-in-law was sick with a high fever, and they spoke to Jesus about her. He went and stood at her bedside and ordered the fever to leave her. The fever left her, and she got up at once and began to wait on them."

LUKE, CHAPTER 4, VERSES 38–39, GOOD NEWS BIBLE

When Jesus heals Simon's mother-in-law, she immediately gets up and begins to serve Jesus and the disciples. It is easy to look harshly on this passage – let the poor woman rest! Yet, Jesus wants to heal us so that we can serve others. That is his message: to love one another. We are made well to love and serve one another.

"She got up at once and began to wait on them."

"Come to me, all of you who are weary and burdened, and I will give you rest."

JESUS, SPEAKING IN MATTHEW, CHAPTER 11, VERSE 28,
CHRISTIAN STANDARD BIBLE

Explore the ancient idea of *accidie*. Known as the "noon day" demon, accidie can be understood as that listless feeling of staring ahead and being unable to do anything.

Female medieval mystic and musician Hildegard von Bingen spoke of the soul being *"weakened by the coldness of indifference and neglect"*. Remember this, and know that feelings of weakness have afflicted great saints throughout the ages. Hildegard encourages all of us to embrace instead the *"fire of the holy spirit"*.

"Above all, do not be ashamed of yourself, for that is the root of your trouble."

FYODOR DOSTOEVSKY, IN *THE BROTHERS KARAMAZOV*.

Consider today why you may feel shame, and then allow yourself the mercy of letting it slip away. *Do not be ashamed of yourself.*

"Not so, not so, no load of woe
Need bring despairing frown;
For while we bear it, we can bear,
Past that, we lay it down."

SARAH WILLIAMS, ENGLISH POET

"Hard words *will* vex; unkindness *will* pierce; neglect *will* wound; threatened evils *will* make the soul quiver; sharp pain or weariness *will* rack the body, or make it restless. But what says the psalmist? 'When my heart is vexed, I will complain.' To whom? Not *of* God, but *to* God."

EDWARD PUSEY, REGIUS PROFESSOR OF HEBREW AT OXFORD

"God never places us in any position in which we cannot grow. We may fancy that He does. We may fear we are so impeded by fretting, petty cares that we are gaining nothing; but when we are not sending any branches upward, we may be sending roots downward. Perhaps in the time of our humiliation, when everything seems a failure, we are making the best kind of progress."

ELIZABETH PRENTISS, AMERICAN AUTHOR

"We are so much more ready to ask for God's blessing than for God's will. That which is often asked of God is not so much God's will and way, as God's approval of our way. We want to have our own path made easy and successful, and we call that asking for God's guidance."

SARAH FRANCES SMILEY, AMERICAN QUAKER

"Let nothing disturb you,
Let nothing frighten you,
All things are passing away:
God never changes.
Patience obtains all things
Whoever has God lacks nothing;
God alone suffices."

SAINT TERESA OF ÁVILA, SPANISH MYSTIC

"Ah, if you knew what peace there is an accepted sorrow."

MADAME GUYON, FRENCH MYSTIC

The profound transition from *resistance* of a calamitous event to *acceptance* of the sorrow can immeasurably help bring paradoxical peace to the sadness. Stop struggling and let the healing process begin.

"God has care for men, he loves the human race, he wishes it well, nothing so true. Yet he allows men to fall, he often allows them to perish, he gives them goods that tend towards their destruction; and when he makes someone happy, it is after many sufferings: where is his affection, where is his goodness or again where is his power? …[These objections] ignore the fact that it is of God one speaks. It is as though one were speaking of a mother, a guardian, a tutor, whose well-nigh only care is concerned with the upbringing, the preservation, the happiness of the person in question, and who neglect their duty. God takes care of the universe, he neglects nothing, he chooses what is best on the whole."

GOTTFRIED LEIBNITZ, GERMAN PHILOSOPHER

PRAISE AND THANKSGIVING

I will magnify You, O Lord.
You have exalted me and have
not made my foes to rejoice over me.
O Lord, my God, I cried to you;
and you have restored me.
O Lord, you have brought up
my soul out of the grave.
You have revived me from those
who go down into the pit.

PSALM 30, VERSES 1–3

"For my thoughts are not your thoughts, nor are your ways, says the Lord. For as the heavens are higher than the earth, so are my ways, higher than your ways, and my thoughts than your thoughts. For as the rain and the snow come down from heaven, and do not return there until they have watered the earth, making it bring forth and sprout, giving seed to the sower and bread to the eater, so shall my word be that goes out from my mouth; it shall not return to me empty, but it shall accomplish that which I purpose, and succeed in the thing for which I sent it."

ISAIAH, CHAPTER 55, VERSES 8-11, NEW REVISED STANDARD VERSION

Never underestimate the immensity of the Lord!

"This is the day that the Lord has made;
Let us rejoice and be glad in it.
Save us, we pray, O Lord!
O Lord, we pray, give us success!"

PSALM 118, VERSES 24–25

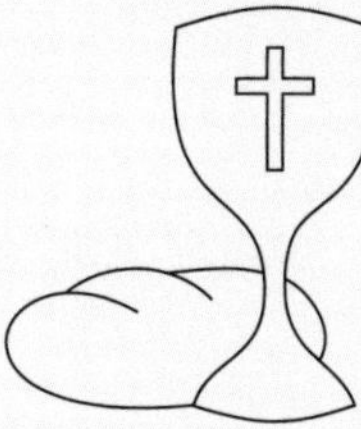

"Enjoy the blessings of this day, if God sends them; and bear patiently the thorns. For this day is only ours, we are dead to yesterday, and we are not yet born tomorrow."

JEREMY TAYLOR, ENGLISH CLERIC

"You have given so much to me,
Give one thing more, a grateful heart.
Not thankful when it pleases me,
As if your blessings had spare days;
But such a heart, whose pulse may
be your praise."

GEORGE HERBERT, ENGLISH POET

Contemplate the image of your heart's pulse being one of praise to God. With each unknowing beat, praise is being pulsed around the body.

"On a wintry night, if you gaze upon the sky and see stars upon stars, and without end, and consider that many of these stars are very much larger than this earth of ours whereon we live, and that behind the stars which we see there are hundreds, thousands, millions of stars as large and larger even, and that there is no end to the stars and the heavens, you must realize that there is something which you cannot grasp."

"But if we look within our own self, and sense there that which we call our soul, when we see within our own self something that we likewise fail to grasp, but something which we know more assuredly than anything else, and through which we know all that is, then we see even in our own soul something still more incomprehensible, something still greater than that which we see in the heavens.

That which we see in the heavens and sense within our own soul is the very thing we call God."

LEO TOLSTOY, FROM *THE WAY OF LIFE*

*"Rejoice in the Lord always;
and again I say, 'Rejoice!'"*

PHILIPPIANS, CHAPTER 4, VERSE 4, 21ST-CENTURY KING JAMES BIBLE

Try divine deep breathing
Inhale deeply, maintain you inhalation for 10 seconds and breathe out slowly. Take the breath in deeper and on each slow exhalation allow yourself to rejoice. Smile in between breaths. Allow the joy of Christ to infuse your entire body.

14 AUGUST

JUSTICE

"Don't be upset because of evil people.
Don't be jealous of those who do wrong,
because like the grass, they will soon dry up.
Like green plants, they will soon die away."

PSALM 37, VERSES 1-2, NEW CENTURY VERSION

"To him who strikes you on the one cheek, offer the other also. And from him who takes away your cloak, do not withhold your tunic either. Give to everyone who asks of you. And from him who takes away your goods do not ask them back."

JESUS SPEAKING DURING THE SERMON ON THE MOUNT, LUKE, CHAPTER 6, VERSES 29–30, NEW KING JAMES VERSION.

"O Jesus! True liberty of angels, paradise of delights, remember the horror and sadness which you did endure when your enemies, like furious lions, surrounded you, and by thousands of insults, spits, blows, lacerations and other unheard-of cruelties, tormented you at will. In consideration of these torments and insulting words, I beg you, O my Savior, to deliver me from all my enemies, visible and invisible, and to bring me, under your protection, to the perfection of eternal salvation. Amen."

SAINT BRIDGET OF SWEDEN, CATHOLIC MYSTIC

For everything there is a season,
and a time for every activity under heaven.

A time to be born, and a time to die;
a time to plant, and a time to uproot
what is planted.

A time to kill, and a time to heal;
a time to tear down, and a time to build up.

A time to weep, and a time to laugh;
a time to mourn, and a time to dance.

A time to scatter stones,
and a time to gather them;
a time to embrace,
and a time to refrain from embracing.

A time to seek, and a time to lose;
a time to keep, and a time to discard.

A time to tear, and a time to mend;
a time to be silent, and a time to speak.

A time to love, and a time to hate:
a time for war, and a time for peace.

ECCLESIASTES, CHAPTER 3, VERSES ONE-EIGHT, NEW CATHOLIC BIBLE

"And the effect of righteousness will be peace, and the result of righteousness, quietness and trust for ever."

ISAIAH, CHAPTER 32, VERSES 17, REVISED STANDARD VERSION

"The salvation of the righteous comes
from the Lord;
he is their stronghold in time of trouble.
The Lord helps them and delivers them;
he delivers them from the wicked and
saves them,
because they take refuge in him."

PSALM 37, VERSES 39–40, NEW INTERNATIONAL VERSION

"The prayer of a righteous person has great power as it is working."

JAMES, CHAPTER 5, VERSE 16,
ENGLISH STANDARD VERSION

"He shall come down like rain upon
the grass before mowing,
Like showers that water the earth.
In His days the righteous shall flourish,
And abundance of peace,
Until the moon is no more."

A PSALM OF SOLOMON, PSALM 72, VERSES 6-7, NEW KING JAMES VERSION

"O Lord, in whom all things live, who commands us to seek You and are ready to be found; to know You is life, to serve You is freedom, to praise You is our souls' joy. We bless You, and adore You, we worship You and glorify You, we give thanks to You for Your great glory."

SAINT AUGUSTINE, 4TH-CENTURY CHURCH FATHER

When gratitude bubbles up in our hearts, let it sing out with joy. And when joy feels out of reach, contemplate the notion that *to praise You is our souls' joy.*

"Then our mouth was filled with laughter, and our tongue with shouts of joy; then they said among the nations, 'The Lord has done great things for them.'"

PSALM 126, VERSE 2, ENGLISH STANDARD VERSION

Be joyful today! Show others what marvellous things have been given to you.

"O Lord, I give you humble and hearty thanks for your great goodness and mercy towards me. What you have planned for me to do or to suffer, you alone know. Give me patience and courage, and a firm resolution to do your service, and the grace to do it."

ARCHBISHOP LAUD, ARCHBISHOP OF CANTERBURY

I relied completely on the Lord,
and he turned towards me
and heard my cry for help.
He lifted me out of the watery pit,
out of the slimy mud.
He placed my feet on a rock
and gave me secure footing.
He gave me reason to sing a new song,
praising our God.

PSALM 40, VERSES 1–3, NEW ENGLISH TRANSLATION

Prayerful action:
focus carefully on this couplet.

He placed my feet on a rock
and gave me secure footing.

"Love all men, love everything. Seek that rapture and ecstasy. Water the earth with the tears of your joy and love those tears."

FYODOR DOSTOEVSKY, *IN THE BROTHERS KARAMAZOV*

Read and repeat until you can hear the voice of the divine in your heart.

"Lord, You have been our habitation
from generation to generation.
Before the mountains were made (and
you had formed the Earth and the world),
even from everlasting to everlasting,
You are God."

PSALM 90, VERSES 1-3, REVISED GENEVA TRANSLATION

"Let us, then, always offer praise to God as our sacrifice through Jesus, which is the offering presented by lips that confess him as Lord. Do not forget to do good and to help one another, because these are the sacrifices that please God."

HEBREWS, CHAPTER 13, VERSES 15–16, GOOD NEWS BIBLE

UNITY WITH ONE ANOTHER

"O God, make up the disagreements which divide us from each other. Bring us back into a unity of love which reflects your divine nature. And, as you are *above all things*, make us united by the unanimity of a good mind, that through the embrace of love and the ties of affection, we may be spiritually one, as well in ourselves, as in each other."

DIONYSIUS OF THE SYRIAN JACOBITE CHURCH

"I therefore, a prisoner for the Lord, urge you to walk in a manner worthy of the calling to which you have been called, with all humility and gentleness, with patience, bearing with one another in love, eager to maintain the unity of the Spirit in the bond of peace."

SAINT PAUL, CHAPTER 4, VERSES 1–3, ENGLISH STANDARD VERSION

"And above all things have fervent love for one another, for 'love will cover a multitude of sins.'"

IN 1 PETER, CHAPTER 4, VERSE 8, NEW KING JAMES VERSION

Friendships fray, families fracture, colleagues collide. What is the answer to all of this? Jesus and his apostles are very clear: *to love one another*. This command is shared repeatedly in the New Testament, directly from Jesus and from his apostles. Are we wiser than they to ignore it? What is the answer then? *To love one another*.

"There is one body and one Spirit, just as you were called to one hope when you were called, one Lord, one faith, one baptism, one God and Father of all, who is over all and through all and in all."

EPHESIANS, CHAPTER 4, VERSES 4-7, NEW INTERNATIONAL VERSION

Avoid the clamour of petty squabbling and remember the unity of the body of Christ, both here and in heaven.

"Where there is no love, put love, and you will draw out love."

SAINT JOHN OF THE CROSS, SPANISH MYSTIC

"Those who belong to Christ Jesus have nailed the passions and desires of their sinful nature to his cross and crucified them there. Since we are living by the spirit, let us follow the spirit's leading in every part of our lives. Let us not become conceited, or provoke one another, or be jealous of one another."

GALATIANS, CHAPTER 5, VERSES 24–26, NEW LIVING TRANSLATION

"Small kindnesses, small courtesies, small considerations, habitually practised in our social intercourse, give a greater charm to the character than the display of great talents and accomplishments."

MARY ANNE KELTY, ENGLISH WRITER

"O Lord, who gave the disciples peace, shine down upon us all your holy calm; gather together with your hand all those who are scattered, and bring them like sheep into the fold of your holy Church, through Jesus Christ our Lord."

THEODORE STUDITE, BYZANTINE MONK

"Jesus took with him Peter, James, and John, and led them up a high mountain, where they were alone. As they looked on, a change came over Jesus, and his clothes became shining white – whiter than anyone in the world could wash them. Then the three disciples saw Elijah and Moses talking with Jesus."

MARK, CHAPTER 9, VERSES 2–4, GOOD NEWS BIBLE

Known as the Transfiguration, Jesus is "transfigured", changed, and his divine nature is revealed. God speaks and says, *"This is my own dear Son – listen to him!"* The divine strangeness of the episode continues to surprise us today. Jesus is no mere wise man, or kindly teacher. His nature is divine and we are commanded to *listen to him!*

FINDING SALVATION

Whoever you may be, always
have God before your eyes,
Whatever you do, do it according to
the testimony of the holy Scriptures,
In whatever place you live,
do not easily leave it.

Keep these three precepts
and you will be saved.

SAINT ANTHONY, EGYPTIAN HERMIT

"The Lord also will be a refuge for the oppressed, a refuge in times of trouble."

PSALM NINE, VERSE NINE, 21ST-CENTURY KING JAMES BIBLE

If you are a beginner in faith and trying to live in love, let these words of comfort wash over you. Be soothed by their promise of protection and care for your wellbeing.

When we turn away from some duty or some fellow-creature, saying that our hearts are too sick and sore with some great yearning of our own, we may often sever the line on which a divine message was coming to us…There is a plan working in our lives; and if we keep our hearts quiet and our eyes open, it all works together; and if we don't, it all fights together, and goes on fighting till it comes right, somehow, somewhere.

ANNIE KEARY, NOVELIST WHO HELPED TO RUN A VICTORIAN HOME FOR UNEMPLOYED SERVANT GIRLS

"I am the light of the world. The one who follows me will never walk in darkness, but will have the light of life."

JESUS SPEAKING IN JOHN, CHAPTER EIGHT, VERSE 12, INTERNATIONAL STANDARD VERSION

Celebrate the joy of finding wisdom

Joyful is the person who finds wisdom,
the one who gains understanding.

For wisdom is more profitable than silver,
and her wages are better than gold.

Wisdom is more precious than rubies;
nothing you desire can compare with her.

She offers you long life in her right hand,
and riches and honour in her left.

She will guide you down delightful paths;
all her ways are satisfying.

Wisdom is a tree of life to those who
embrace her;
happy are those who hold her tightly.

PROVERBS, CHAPTER THREE, VERSES 13–18, NEW LIVING TRANSLATION

"Turn often to our Lord who is watching you, poor frail little being as you are, amongst your work and distractions. He sends you help, and blesses your affliction. This thought should enable you to bear your troubles patiently and gently, for love of God who only allows you to be tried for your own good. Raise your heart continually to God, see his aid, and let the foundation stone of your consolation be your happiness in being his. All troubles and annoyances will be comparatively unimportant while you know that you have such a friend, such a support, such a protector."

FRANCIS DE SALES, BISHOP OF GENEVA

"I am the light of the world."

JOHN, CHAPTER 8, VERSE 12, ENGLISH STANDARD VERSION

Prayerful contemplation:
Is your light dimming or brightening?
Whose light can you kindle today?
How can your light glean heat and
warmth from the light of Christ?

"The Lord hears those who cry out,
and he delivers them from all their distress.
The Lord is close to the brokenhearted,
and he delivers those whose spirit has
been crushed.
A righteous person will have many troubles,
but the Lord will deliver him from them all.
God protects all his bones;
not one of them will be broken."

PSALM 34, VERSES 17–20, INTERNATIONAL STANDARD VERSION

A woman who had been bleeding for 12 years found it difficult to get close to Jesus as the crowds surrounding him were so great. She reached instead just to touch the hem of his clothes.

"For she said, 'If I touch even his garments, I will be made well.' And immediately the flow of blood dried up, and she felt in her body that she was healed of her disease.
And Jesus, perceiving in himself that power had gone out from him… he said to her, 'Daughter, your faith has made you well; go in peace, and be healed of your disease.'"

MARK, CHAPTER 5, VERSES 28–24, ENGLISH STANDARD VERSION

"Daughter, your faith has made you well."

Contemplate whether a connection exists between faith in Christ and wellness. What connection have you discovered between a settled mind orientated towards the Lord and a well body?

"It has been well said that no one ever sank under the burden of the day. It is when tomorrow's burden is added to the burden of today that the weight is more than a person can bear. Never load yourself so, my friends… God begs you to leave the future to Him."

GEORGE MACDONALD, SCOTTISH MINISTER

"If you hold to my teaching, you are really my disciples. Then you will know the truth, and the truth will set you free."

JESUS SPEAKING IN JOHN, CHAPTER 8, VERSE 31, NEW INTERNATIONAL VERSION

If you like this passage, share it. Create a picture quote and send to friend. Pin on the refrigerator, next to the bathroom mirror, your laptop screen saver. Words are not lifeless, but they do need to be read, understood, and spoken, to live.

"Hold to my teaching."

Are you holding to Jesus's command
to love your enemy?
Are you holding to Jesus's command
to love your neighbour?
Are you holding to Jesus's command
to forgive?

"I've been a great deal happier since I have given up thinking about what is easy and pleasant, and being discontented because I couldn't have my own way. Our life is determined for us; and it makes the mind very free when we give up wishing, and only think of bearing what is laid upon us, and doing what is given us to do."

GEORGE ELIOT, FROM *MILL ON THE FLOSS*

What has been given us to do today? Can we do it with glad hearts and our full attention?

“Be strong to hope, O heart!
Though day is bright,
The stars can only shine
In the dark night.
Be strong, O heart of mine,
Look towards the light!”

ADELAIDE ANNE PROCTER, ENGLISH POET

"I alone know the plans I have for you, plans to bring you prosperity and not disaster, plans to bring about the future you hope for."

JEREMIAH, CHAPTER 29, VERSE 11, GOOD NEWS BIBLE

It is said that the way to heaven is through prayer. Start small and whisper these words.

"To live a Godly life is to be like unto God. To be like unto God, you must fear nothing and desire nothing for self. In order to fear nothing and desire nothing for self, you need only love.

Some say, look within, and you will have peace. This is not the entire truth.

Others say: come out of self; strive to forget self and seek happiness in pleasures. This also is untrue. This is untrue if alone for the reason that pleasures will not eliminate disease. Peace and happiness are neither within us, nor outside of us, but are in God, and God is both within us and outside of us.

Love God, and you will find in God that which you seek."

LEO TOLSTOY, FROM *THE WAY OF LIFE*

WORK

"You are the light of the world. A city that is set on a hill cannot be hidden. Nor do they light a lamp and put it under a basket, but on a lampstand, and it gives light to all who are in the house. Let your light so shine before men, that they may see your good works and glorify your Father in heaven."

JESUS'S WORDS WITHIN THE SERMON ON THE MOUNT, MATTHEW, CHAPTER 5, VERSES 14–16, NEW KING JAMES VERSION

"As each one has received a gift, minister it to one another, as good stewards of the manifold grace of God."

1 PETER, CHAPTER 4, VERSE 10, NEW KING JAMES VERSION

"For no good tree bears bad fruit, nor again does a bad tree bear good fruit, for each tree is known by its own fruit. For figs are not gathered from thorns, nor are grapes picked from brambles."

JESUS SPEAKING IN LUKE, CHAPTER 6, VERSES 43–44, NEW ENGLISH TRANSLATION

You shall know them by their fruits.

This concept is a central theme within Christianity: there is a connection between genuine faith, spiritual endeavour and external “fruits” – the visible outcomes of one’s character and actions. Just as a rotten tree won’t bear fruit, neither will a withered soul flourish.

What are examples of “good fruit” in your life as a believer?

"Look up and not down,
Look forward and not back,
Look out and not in,
And lend a hand."

EDWARD E. HALE, AMERICAN MINISTER

"One of those listening was a woman from the city of Thyatira named Lydia, a dealer in purple cloth. She was a worshiper of God. The Lord opened her heart to respond to Paul's message. When she and the members of her household were baptized, she invited us to her home. 'If you consider me a believer in the Lord,' she said, 'come and stay at my house.' And she persuaded us."

SAINT LUKE, ACTS OF THE APOSTLES, CHAPTER 16, VERSES 14–16, NEW INTERNATIONAL VERSION

Be inspired by Lydia, a dealer in purple cloth and remember that the message of the Gospels is for all women – not just the meek and mild. Purple cloth was a luxury item in the ancient world; to act as a dealer, Lydia would have been an astute business woman. Lydia, a dealer in purple cloth, invited the apostles into her home and gave them shelter.

"Does the road wind up-hill all the way?
Yes to the very end.
Will the journey take the whole long day?
From morn to night, my friend."

CHRISTINA ROSSETTI, ENGLISH POET

Modern managerial speak would explain this poem as *expectation management*. Once we realize our life on earth will be akin to the slow long uphill walk – with many hopeful stops along the way to experience deep joy, love and happiness – we can better understand how best to approach the heavenly path.

"Lord, let me not live to be useless."

JOHN WESLEY, FATHER OF METHODISM

Jesus said *"blessed are the poor in spirit"*; never be ashamed when feeling useless or fearing uselessness.

"Lord, I do not pray for tasks equal to my strength: I ask for strength equal to my task."

PHILLIPS BROOKS, AMERICAN CLERGYMAN

"Try, in the presence of God, to know yourself. Then seek to know for what God sent you into the world; how have you fulfilled it; do you know yet what God wants you to be; what is God's will for you now; what thing can you do now?… Say to God, 'Teach me to do your will, for you are my God,' and he will say to your soul, 'Fear not; I am your salvation.'"

E.B. PUSEY, ENGLISH THEOLOGIAN

"I have set you an example that you should do as I have done for you. Very truly I tell you, no servant is greater than his master, nor is a messenger greater than the one who sent him. Now that you know these things, you will be blessed if you do them."

JESUS SPEAKING IN JOHN, CHAPTER 13, VERSE 15

By washing his disciples' feet, Jesus presents the ultimate example of servanthood. How do we serve, whom do we serve? Is our humility genuine?

She selects wool and flax
and works with eager hands.

She is like the merchant ships,
bringing her food from afar.

She gets up while it is still night;
she provides food for her family
and portions for her female servants.

She considers a field and buys it;
out of her earnings she plants a vineyard.

She sets about her work vigorously;
her arms are strong for her tasks.

She sees that her trading is profitable,
and her lamp does not go out at night.

PROVERBS, CHAPTER 31, VERSES 13–18, NEW INTERNATIONAL VERSION

Meet the *"woman of noble character"* in Proverbs, chapter 31. She is the original having-it-all and doing-it-all woman: trading, cooking, hosting, running a household. Are we, too, able to *"set about"* our work *"vigorously"*? Are we, too, able to *"work with eager hands"*?

BEING MOVED BY GOD

American Trappist monk Thomas Merton experienced a transcendent moment in an ordinary shopping district. Be alive therefore to the divine in the everyday.

In Louisville, at the corner of Fourth and Walnut, in the center of the shopping district, I was suddenly overwhelmed with the realization that I loved all those people, that they were mine and I theirs, that we could not be alien to one another even though we were total strangers… This sense of liberation from an illusory difference was such a relief and such a joy to me that I almost laughed out loud… And if only everybody could realize this! But it cannot be explained. There is no way of telling people that they are all walking around shining like the sun.

THOMAS MERTON, *CONJECTURES OF A GUILTY BYSTANDER*

"Our body is weak, unclean, mortal, but a treasure is concealed in it, the immortal spirit of God. If we but recognize this spirit within us, we shall love our fellow man, and if we love our fellow man, we shall attain all that our heart desires: we shall be happy."

HRYHORII SKOVORODA, UKRAINIAN PHILOSOPHER

"Blessed Lord, grant to such a measure of your spirit so we may follow you in all self-denial and tenderness of soul. Help us, by your great love, to support the afflicted, to relieve the needy and destitute, to comfort the feeble-hearted, to share the burdens of the heavy laden and always to see You in all who are poor and desolate."

DR WESTCOTT, BISHOP OF CALCUTTA

Today, whose heavy burdens may we seek to share?
Today, how shall we love the afflicted?
Today, how may we give comfort?

"May thy mercy be extended over all mankind, bringing the ignorant to the knowledge of thy truth, awakening the impenitent, touching the hardened. Look with compassion upon the afflicted of every condition, assuage the pangs of disease, comfort the broken in spirit."

JANE AUSTEN, FROM *ANOTHER DAY IS NOW GONE*

Modern Living

"All the widows stood around him, crying and showing him the robes and other clothing that Tabitha had made while she was still with them."

ACTS, CHAPTER 9, VERSE 39, NEW INTERNATIONAL VERSION

Saint Peter is taken to see the dead body of Tabitha, a clothes maker. He raises her from the dead and this miracle helps spread the good news of Christ around the cosmopolitan city of Joppa. Tabitha, with her beautifully made clothes, was *"always doing good and helping the poor."*

Be inspired by Tabitha and use what influence you have to spread the Good News.

"We tarnish the lustre of our most beautiful actions when we applaud them ourselves."

HÉLOÏSE D'ARGENTEUIL, 12TH-CENTURY SCHOLAR

Do you agree with Héloïse?
How should we best celebrate ourselves?
Can an overuse of social media self-promotion tarnish that which deserves praise?

"No one can serve two masters, because either he will hate one and love the other, or be loyal to one and despise the other. You cannot serve God and riches!"

JESUS SPEAKING IN MATTHEW, CHAPTER 6, VERSE 24, INTERNATIONAL STANDARD VERSION

"And [Jesus] called the people to him again and said to them, 'Hear me, all of you, and understand: There is nothing outside a person that by going into him can defile him, but the things that come out of a person are what defile him.'"

JESUS SPEAKING IN MARK, CHAPTER 7, VERSES 14–15, ENGLISH STANDARD VERSION

"There is nothing outside a person that by going into him can defile him, but the things that come out of a person are what defile him."

JESUS SPEAKING IN MARK, CHAPTER 7, VERSES 14–15, ENGLISH STANDARD VERSION

Clean eating, five-a-day, Veganuary, keto diets, juice cleanses, detoxes, Paleo eating, all may have their place, but we are reminded that we are spoiled, not by what we put into our bodies, but by what comes out: our actions and our words.

"Truth is so obscure in these times, and falsehood so established, that unless we love the truth, we cannot know it."

BLAISE PASCAL, FRENCH PHILOSOPHER

Do not be afraid to question all current ideologies that are presented as being the truth. Consider carefully all things that are presented as fact and establish within your heart whether they are true or false, remembering the words of Christ: *"I am the way, the truth and the life."*

"A mind is free when it protects itself against the intrusions of society, and does not cower to human opinion. A free mind refuses to be the slave or tool of the many or of the few. A free mind guards its empire over itself as nobler than the empire of the world."

WILLIAM ELLERY CHANNING, AMERICAN PREACHER

"You are like whitewashed tombs, which look fine on the outside but are full of bones and decaying corpses on the inside. In the same way, on the outside you appear good to everybody, but inside you are full of hypocrisy and sins."

JESUS SPEAKING IN MATTHEW, CHAPTER 23, VERSES 27–28, GOOD NEWS TRANSLATION

What do we value more, externalities or internal goodness? What more could be done to redress the balance?

"Detach yourself from the love of the multitude in case your enemies question your spirit and trouble your inner peace."

DIOSCORUS, 4TH-CENTURY POPE OF ALEXANDRIA

Christian faith does not exclude the use of human reason. Put your mind to this passage. *What does it mean? Is it true? Does it make sense? How does it make you feel? Does it resonate with you?* If so, repeat the passage and let it settle within your mind's library.

Avoid complaining about, 'your birth, your training, your employment your hardship', avoid fancying that you could be something if only you had a different lot and sphere assigned to you. God understands his own plan, and he knows what you want a great deal better than you do. The very things that you most deprecate, as fatal limitations or obstructions are probably what you most want. What you call hindrances, obstacles, discouragements are probably God's opportunities.'

HORACE BUSHELL, AMERICAN PREACHER

"Just as a treasure that is exposed loses its value, so a virtue which is known vanishes; just as wax melts when it is near fire, so the soul is destroyed by praise and loses all the results of its labour."

SYNCLETICA OF ALEXANDRIA, 4TH-CENTURY DESERT MOTHER

"No foul language should come from your mouth, but only what is good for building up someone in need, so that it gives grace to those who hear."

EPHESIANS, CHAPTER 4, VERSE 29, CHRISTIAN STANDARD BIBLE

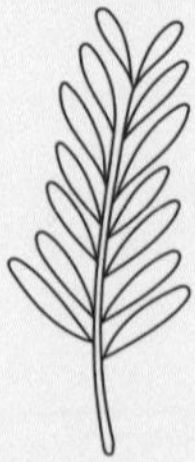

"Whatever is true, whatever is honourable, whatever is just, whatever is pure, whatever is lovely, whatever is commendable – if there is any moral excellence and if there is anything praiseworthy – dwell on these things."

THE PHILIPPIANS, CHAPTER 4, VERSE 8, CHRISTIAN STANDARD BIBLE

"Be careful not to practice your righteousness in front of others to be seen by them. If you do, you will have no reward from your Father in heaven… "When you give to the needy, do not let your left hand know what your right hand is doing, so that your giving may be in secret. Then your Father, who sees what is done in secret, will reward you."

JESUS SPEAKING IN MATTHEW, CHAPTER 6, VERSES 1–4, NEW INTERNATIONAL VERSION

"Be careful not to practice your righteousness in front of others to be seen by them."

Savour this passage and appreciate that Jesus was on to "virtue signalling" over two thousand years ago!

"As Jesus looked up, he saw the rich putting their gifts into the temple treasury. He also saw a poor widow put in two very small copper coins. '*Truly I tell you*,' he said, '*this poor widow has put in more than all the others*.'"

LUKE, CHAPTER 21, VERSES 1–3

Jesus and the story of the widow's mite shows us that it is not *how much*, but *how*, we give to others.

"An unfriendly person pursues selfish ends and against all sound judgment starts quarrels.

Fools find no pleasure in understanding but delight in airing their own opinions."

PROVERBS, CHAPTER 18, VERSES 1–2, NEW INTERNATIONAL VERSION

Be careful what you post online!

"Stop storing up treasures for yourselves on earth, where moths and rust destroy and where thieves break in and steal. But keep on storing up treasures for yourselves in heaven, where moths and rust do not destroy and where thieves do not break in and steal, because where your treasure is, there your heart will be also."

JESUS SPEAKING IN MATTHEW, CHAPTER 6, VERSES 19–21

Jesus has been arrested and his close disciple Peter denied knowing him.

"Immediately the rooster crowed a second time. And Peter remembered how Jesus had said to him, 'Before the rooster crows twice, you will deny me three times.' And he broke down and wept."'

Social inconvenience has caused the best of people to deny Christ. If sensitive to the social cringe involved in sharing thoughts about Christianity, take courage from Peter and remember that even the most loyal of followers fail sometimes.

"To live content with small means;
to seek elegance rather than luxury,
and refinement rather than fashion;
to be worthy, not respectable, and wealthy, not rich;
to study hard, think quietly, talk gently, act frankly;
to listen to stars and birds,
to babes and sages, with open heart;
to bear all cheerfully, do all bravely,
await occasions, hurry never.
In a word, to let the spiritual, unbidden and unconscious,
grow up through the common. This is to be my symphony."

WILLIAM ELLERY CHANNING, AMERICAN PREACHER

RITUALS

"Then took Mary a pound of ointment of spikenard, very costly, and anointed the feet of Jesus, and wiped his feet with her hair: and the house was filled with the odour of the ointment."

JOHN, CHAPTER 12, VERSE 3, KING JAMES BIBLE

When Mary washed Jesus's feet with expensive perfume, the disciples grumbled and wondered if it would be better to sell the perfume and give the money the poor. Remember Jesus's response: *The poor will always be with you, but I will not always be with you*. The rituals involved in honouring Christ deserve our full care and attention.

"After that he poureth water into a bason, and began to wash the disciples' feet, and to wipe them with the towel wherewith he was girded."

JOHN, CHAPTER 13, VERSE 5, KING JAMES BIBLE

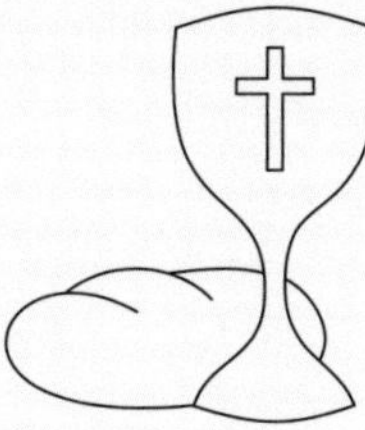

"Lord Jesus, after washing their feet, You commanded Your disciples that they ought to exercise true love and act in sincere humility towards one another. Grant that I may also diligently follow Your example, and since it is not within my power, endow me with Your Holy Spirit, that He might aid me through the power of Your Word, guide me, and protect me from all envy, pride, and arrogance. Amen."

ESAIAS HEIDENREICH, LUTHERAN PREACHER

"And as they did eat, Jesus took the bread, and when he had given thanks, he brake it and gave it to them, and said, 'Take, eat, this is my body.' Also he took the cup, and when he had given thanks, gave it to them: and they all drank of it. And he said unto them, 'This is my blood of that new Testament which is shed for many.'"

JESUS AT THE LAST SUPPER, IN MARK, CHAPTER 14, VERSES 22–24, 1599 GENEVA BIBLE

"One thing alone sustains me and that is Holy Communion. From it I draw all my strength; in it is all my comfort… I would not know how to give glory to God if I did not have the Eucharist in my heart."

SAINT FAUSTINA, POLISH NUN

"Do not let your hearts be distressed. You believe in God; believe also in me. There are many dwelling places in my Father's house."

JESUS AT THE LAST SUPPER, JOHN, CHAPTER 14, VERSES 1–2, NEW ENGLISH TRANSLATION

That Jesus's disciples – men Christ called his *friends* – were *distressed* brings comfort to those who interpret our own distress at Christ's distance as despair. Remember always: *Do not let your hearts be distressed.*

DEATH

"So they took Jesus, and he went out, bearing his own cross, to the place called The Place of a Skull, which in Aramaic is called Golgotha. There they crucified him."

JOHN, CHAPTER 19, VERSE 17, ENGLISH STANDARD VERSION

"In order that we should realize the distance between ourselves and God, it was necessary that God should be a crucified slave. For we do not realize distance except in the downward direction. It is much easier to imagine ourselves in the place of God the Creator than in the place of Christ crucified."

SIMON WEIL, FRENCH PHILOSOPHER

"In a world where success is the measure and justification of all things the figure of Him who was sentenced and crucified remains a stranger and is at best the object of pity … The figure of the Crucified invalidates all thought that takes success for its standard."

DIETRICH BONHOEFFER, GERMAN PASTOR, EXECUTED IN 1945

At the time of the Roman Empire, where might was measured in gold and wars, palaces and strength, the power of God killed on the cross, a gruesome form of execution reserved for the lowest of criminals, continues to shock. In understanding this profound paradox, we are invited to comprehend the whole deep wonder of the Gospel. Victory is to be found, not in conquering and defeat, but love and forgiveness.

The words Jesus Christ said on the cross:

"Father, forgive them,
for they know not what they do."

"Truly, I say to you,
today you will be with me in paradise."

"Woman, behold, your son! …
Behold, your mother!"

"Eli, Eli, lama sabachthani? ('My God,
my God, why have you forsaken me?')"

"I thirst."

"It is finished."

"Father, into your hands I commit my spirit!"

"Watch Lord those who weep tonight,
Give your angels charge over those who sleep.
Tend your sick ones O Lord Christ.
Rest your weary ones,
Bless your dying ones,
Soothe your suffering ones,
Pity your afflicted ones,
Shield your joyous ones,
And all, for your Love's sake."

MARTIN LUTHER, GERMAN THEOLOGIAN

"I believe that I shall see the goodness
of the Lord
in the land of the living.
Wait for the Lord;
be strong and he shall comfort your heart;
wait patiently for the Lord."

PSALM 27, VERSES 13–14, *BOOK OF COMMON PRAYER*

"Good Lord, give me the grace to spend my life in such a way that when the day of my death shall come, though I feel pain in my body, I may feel comfort in my soul; with faithful hope of your mercy, in due love towards you and charity towards the world, I may through your grace, depart into your glory."

SIR THOMAS MORE, ENGLISH STATESMAN AND MARTYR

Am I a stone, and not a sheep,
That I can stand, O Christ, beneath Thy cross,
To number drop by drop Thy blood's slow loss,
And yet not weep?

Not so those women loved
Who with exceeding grief lamented Thee;
Not so fallen Peter, weeping bitterly;
Not so the thief was moved;

Not so the Sun and Moon
Which hid their faces in a starless sky,
A horror of great darkness at broad noon –
I, only I.

Yet give not o'er,
But seek Thy sheep, true Shepherd of the flock;
Greater than Moses, turn and look once more
And smite a rock.

GOOD FRIDAY BY CHRISTINA ROSSETTI

Lamb of God, you take
away the sin of the world,
have mercy on us.

Lamb of God, you take
away the sin of the world,
have mercy on us.

Lamb of God, you take
away the sin of the world,
grant us peace.

The Agnus Dei – the Lamb of God – is based on John the Baptist's short sermon *"Behold, the Lamb of God who takes away the sin of the world."* It has been part of the church liturgy since the 7th century. Seek out a choral version of the passage and find consolation in its beauty.

"I hold out my arms to my Redeemer, who… has come to suffer and to die for me on earth, at the time and under all the circumstances foretold. By His grace, I await death in peace, in the hope of being eternally united to Him."

BLAISE PASCAL, FRENCH PHILOSOPHER

"O God, early in the morning I cry to you.
Help me to pray and gather my thoughts
to you, I cannot do it alone.
In me it is dark, but with you there is light;
I am lonely, but you do not desert me;
My courage fails me, but with you there is help;
I am restless, but with you there is peace;
In me there is bitterness, but with you there
is patience;
I do not understand your ways,
but you know the way for me.
Father in Heaven praise and thanks
be to you for the night."

DIETRICH BONHOEFFER, GERMAN PASTOR

Be O Lord,
a guiding star above me,
a smooth path below me,
a kindly shepherd behind me
and a bright flame before me;
today, tonight and forever. Amen.

A PRAYER OF SAINT COLUMBA

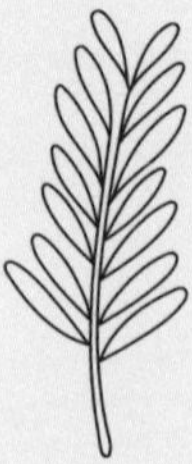

"The Almighty and Merciful God, grant us a quiet night and a perfect end. Amen."

THE FINAL PRAYER OF COMPLINE, AN EVENING SERVICE SAID IN ENGLISH PARISH CHURCHES FOR OVER 500 YEARS.

RESURRECTION

"And, behold, there was a great earthquake: for the angel of the Lord descended from heaven, and came and rolled back the stone from the door, and sat upon it. His countenance was like lightning, and his raiment white as snow… And the angel answered and said unto the women, 'Fear not ye: for I know that ye seek Jesus, which was crucified. He is not here: for he is risen.'"

MATTHEW, CHAPTER 28, VERSES 1–6, KING JAMES BIBLE

He is not here:
for he is risen.

This then in is the great glory of the story of Christianity, that has gripped the world since Jesus preached the gospel in Galilee over 2,000 years ago. Death has been overcome.

He is not here:
for he is risen.

"On the third day the friends of Christ coming at daybreak to the place found the grave empty and the stone rolled away. In varying ways they realized the new wonder; but even they hardly realized that the world had died in the night. What they were looking at was the first day of a new creation, with a new heaven and a new earth; and in a semblance of the gardener God walked again in the garden, in the cool not of the evening but the dawn."

G.K. CHESTERTON, ENGLISH WRITER

"Mary stood crying outside the tomb… then she turned around and saw Jesus standing there… she thought he was the gardener, so she said to him, 'If you took him away, sir, tell me where you have put him, and I will go and get him.' Jesus said to her, 'Mary!' She turned toward him and said in Hebrew, 'Rabboni!'" (This means 'Teacher.')

JOHN, CHAPTER 20, VERSES 14-16, GOOD NEWS BIBLE

"The women are the first at the tomb. They are the first to find it empty. They are the first to hear 'He is not here. He has risen.' They are the first to experience the joy of the Resurrection… and they were also the first to proclaim it."

POPE JOHN PAUL II

Remember always that it was the women coming to anoint the dead body of Jesus who were the first to see the risen Lord. It was to women, doing lowly work, to whom Jesus Christ first revealed himself.

"And there will no longer be any night;
and they will not have need of the light
of a lamp nor the light of the sun,
because the Lord God will illumine them;
and they will reign forever and ever."

REVELATION, CHAPTER 22, VERSE 5

"Now that the common Saviour of all has died on our behalf, we who believe in Christ no longer die, as men died aforetime, in fulfilment of the threat of the law. That condemnation has come to an end; and now that, by the grace of the resurrection, corruption has been banished and done away, we are loosed from our mortal bodies in God's good time for each, so that we may obtain thereby a better resurrection. Like seeds cast into the earth, we do not perish in our dissolution, but like them shall rise again, death having been brought to nought by the grace of the Saviour."

SAINT ATHANASIUS, 4TH-CENTURY CHURCH FATHER

"There, you will receive the comforts of all your work, and have joy for all your sorrow; you must reap what you have sown, even the fruit of all your prayers, and tears, and sufferings... In that place you must wear crowns of gold, and enjoy the perpetual sight and vision of the Holy One, for there you shall see him as he is."

JOHN BUNYAN, THE CELESTIAL CITY, THE DESTINATION IN *THE PILGRIM'S PROGRESS*

"All shall be well, and all shall be well, and all manner of thing shall be well."

JULIAN OF NORWICH, ENGLISH THEOLOGIAN

"Perfect love drives out fear."

1 JOHN, CHAPTER 4, VERSE 18, NEW INTERNATIONAL VERSION

It is said that the way to heaven is through prayer. Start small and whisper these words.

"Heaven and earth shall pass away: but my words shall not pass away."

MATTHEW, CHAPTER 24, VERSE 35, GENEVA BIBLE

The latest scholarly debate suggests that the Gospel of Matthew was written only a few decades after the resurrection of Christ. Millennia later, Jesus's words have still not passed away.

"Jesus, said to Thomas, 'Put your finger here, and see my hands; and put out your hand, and place it in my side. Do not disbelieve, but believe.' Thomas answered him, 'My Lord and my God!' Jesus said to him, 'Have you believed because you have seen me? Blessed are those who have not seen and yet have believed.'"

JOHN, CHAPTER 20, VERSES 26–29, ENGLISH STANDARD VERSION

"Blessed are those who have not seen and yet have believed."

Jesus recognized the commitment of faith that is needed to fully appreciate his message. When experiencing doubt, remember Doubting Thomas and understand you are not alone.

*"No one has seen God at any time.
If we love one another, God abides in us,
and His love has been perfected in us."*

1 JOHN, CHAPTER 4, VERSE 12, NEW KING JAMES VERSION

"Everything comes from love, all is ordained for the salvation of man, God does nothing without this in mind. The soul, seeing this, cannot help but be drunk with joy. By the Resurrection, He has made us children of light and given us back the inheritance of heaven."

CATHERINE OF SIENA, ITALIAN MYSTIC

DEIFICATION OF A LIFE IN CHRIST

"And he said unto them, Go ye into all the world, and preach the gospel to every creature."

JESUS SPEAKING IN MARK, CHAPTER 16, VERSE 15, KING JAMES BIBLE

"When the day of Pentecost arrived, they were all together in one place. And suddenly there came from heaven a sound like a mighty rushing wind, and it filled the entire house where they were sitting. And divided tongues as of fire appeared to them and rested on each one of them. And they were all filled with the Holy Spirit and began to speak in other tongues as the Spirit gave them utterance."

ACTS, CHAPTER 2, VERSES 1-4, ENGLISH STANDARD VERSION

"For to one is given through the Spirit the utterance of wisdom, and to another the utterance of knowledge according to the same Spirit, to another faith by the same Spirit, to another gifts of healing by the one Spirit, to another the working of miracles, to another prophecy, to another the ability to distinguish between spirits, to another various kinds of tongues, to another the interpretation of tongues. All these are empowered by one and the same Spirit, who apportions to each one individually as he wills."

CORINTHIANS, CHAPTER 12, VERSES 8-10, ENGLISH STANDARD VERSION

"For in him we live,
and move,
and have our being."

ACTS, CHAPTER 17, VERSE 28, AMERICAN STANDARD VERSION

"For in him we live,
and move,
and have our being."

Holy Spirit, come into my heart;
draw it to you by your power, O my God,
and grant me charity with filial fear.
Preserve me, O beautiful love,
from every evil thought;
warm me, inflame me with your dear love,
and every pain will seem light to me.
My Father, my sweet Lord,
help me in all my actions.
Jesus, love, Jesus, love. Amen.

SAINT CATHERINE OF SIENA, ITALIAN MYSTIC

Discover the eastern orthodox concept of *theosis*. Translated as *deification*, theosis is such that people are joined with God in a bond of love. By taking on a human body, Jesus deified human nature, breaking the barrier between creator and created.

"He has granted to us his precious and very great promises, so that through them you may become partakers of the divine nature."

2 PETER, CHAPTER 1, VERSES 3–4, ENGLISH STANDARD VERSION

"As all of us reflect the glory of the Lord with unveiled faces, we are becoming more like him with ever-increasing glory by the Lord's Spirit."

2 CORINTHIANS, CHAPTER 3, VERSE 18, INTERNATIONAL STANDARD VERSION

"From about half-past ten at night until about half-past midnight, FIRE. … Certitude. Certitude. Feeling. Joy. Peace. GOD of Jesus Christ… Joy, joy, joy, tears of joy."

BLAISE PASCAL, FRENCH PHILOSOPHER DESCRIBING HIS *NIGHT OF FIRE*

"God is here! God is here! ... I began to feel such a love in my soul that I was so happy I did not know what to do with myself. I felt as if I was out of the world, and everything I looked at seemed to be full of God."

SOJOURNER TRUTH, AMERICAN EMANCIPATIONIST

"In the evening, I felt my heart strangely warmed. I felt I did trust in Christ, Christ alone for salvation; and an assurance was given me that He had taken away my sins."

JOHN WESLEY, FOUNDER OF METHODISM

Whether through a powerful mystical experience or the *strange warming of your heart*, be alert to the bodily changes that a commitment to Christianity can bring. There are hundreds of thousands of beautiful testimonies of people describing a peace that pervades the heart, a stilling of the senses, and joy in extreme form. Give yourself permission to be deified.

The Holy Spirit Prayer of Saint Augustine

Breathe in me, O Holy Spirit,
that my thoughts may all be holy.
Act in me, O Holy Spirit,
that my work, too, may be holy.
Draw my heart, O Holy Spirit,
that I love but what is holy.
Strengthen me, O Holy Spirit,
that I may defend all that is holy.
Guard me, then, O Holy Spirit,
that I always may be holy. Amen.

"Holy Spirit, the life that gives life:
You are the cause of all movement.
You are the breath of all creatures.
You are the salve that purifies our souls.
You are the ointment that heals our wounds.
You are the fire that warms our hearts.
You are the light that guides our feet.
Let all the world praise you."

HILDEGARD VON BINGEN, GERMAN NUN

"And the Word became flesh and dwelt among us, and we have seen his glory, glory as of the only Son from the Father, full of grace and truth."

JOHN, CHAPTER 1, VERSE 14, ENGLISH STANDARD VERSION

You are God: we praise you;
You are God: we acclaim you;
You are the eternal Father:
All creation worships you.
To you all angels, all the powers of heaven,
Cherubim and Seraphim, sing in endless praise:
Holy, holy, holy, Lord, God of power and might,
Heaven and earth are full of your glory.

THE OPENING OF THE *TE DEUM* (WE PRAISE YOU O GOD),
A PRAYER OF PRAISE AND GRATITUDE FROM 500AD.

"Christ the light of the world has come to dispel the darkness of our hearts."

CHURCH OF ENGLAND LITURGY

Remember that at its heart, the Christan message is simple. During dark winter months especially, cherish the light that Jesus brings.

"O God, who through the grace of adoption chose us to be children of the light, grant, we pray, that we may not be wrapped in the darkness of error but always be seen to stand in the bright light of truth."

TRADITIONAL CATHOLIC PRAYER FROM THE ROMAN MISSAL

How wonderful it is to be considered 'children of the light'. What does this term mean to you? How ought we to share the light of our love?

"For the one who is ascending never stands still, passing from one beginning to another by means of beginnings that are never ending. The soul never halts in its upward movement... for the desire of the soul that rises ever higher is never sated by what it has already attained."

GREGORY OF NYSSA, ORTHODOX SAINT

"Scripture brought me to the Gate of Paradise, and the mind stood in wonder as it entered."

EPHREM THE SYRIAN, 4TH-CENTURY THEOLOGIAN

If the verses within this little book have given you solace or joy or the spirit of inquiry, continue reading. Seek out the Bible, books of prayers, collections of hymns and poems. Divinely inspired wisdom needs to be read and spoken, memorised and cherished. Let the words of Christian love, live within you.

"Your life as a Christian should make non-believers question their disbelief in God."

DIETRICH BONHOEFFER, GERMAN PASTOR

VOCABULARY

Amen, from Hebrew meaning *truly, so be it, or it is certain*

Angel, from the Greek meaning, *divine messenger*

Christ, from the Greek meaning, *anointed one*

Emmanuel / Immanuel, from Hebrew meaning *God with us*

Eucharist, from the Greek meaning *thanksgiving*

Halleluiah, from the Hebrew meaning *praise the Lord*

Hosanna, *Save us we pray*, a Hebrew appeal for deliverance

Jesus, from the Greek form of Joshua and the Hebrew Yeshua, Jesus means *Saviour*

Messiah, from the Hebrew meaning *anointed one*.

Testament, a *promise between God and man*

BIBLIOGRAPHY

A Simple Way to Pray, Martin Luther, 1535

A Serious Call to a Devout and Holy Life, William Law, 1729

Aurora Leigh, Elizabeth Barratt Browning, 1857

Brothers Karamazov, Dostoevsky, first published 1880

Conjectures of a Guilty Bystander, Thomas Merton, 1996

Diary: Divine Mercy in My Soul, Saint Maria Faustina Kowalska, Marian Press, 1990

Gravity and Grace, Simone Weil, GP Putnam's Sons, 1952

Hildegard of Bingen: Selected Writings, Penguin, 2001

Legends and Lyrics: A Book of Verses, Adelaide Anne Procter, 1858

Letters of Samuel Rutherford, Rev Andrew Bonar

Life of Moses, Gregory of Nyssa, c.390AD

Little Prayer Book, Martin Luther, 1522

On the Incarnation of the Word, Saint Athanasius, St Vladimir's Seminary Press, 1977

Pascal's Pensées, ed. E.P. Dutton, 1958

Perpetual Peace, Immanuel Kant, 1795

Prayers and Meditations, Dr Samuel Johnson, 1785

Prayers of the Middle Ages, Light from a Thousand years, ed. J. Manning Potts, 1908

Reminiscences of Thoughts and Feeling, Mary Anne Kelty, 1852

Revelations of Divine Love, Julian of Norwich, 1373

Selected Sermons of John Henry Newman

Stepping Heavenward, Elizabeth Prentiss, 1869

Talks Among my Flowers, Sarah Frances Smiley, 1880

The 15 prayers of Saint Bridget, first published 14th century

The Bible Reader's Encyclopaedia and Concordance, Rev W.M. Clow, Collins, 1962

The Book of Margery Kempe, first published 1438

The Complete Poems of Christina Rossetti, Louisiana State University Press, 1979

The Dialogue of Saint Catherine of Siena, first published 1472

The Everlasting Man, G.K. Chesterton, 1925

The Exemplary Life of the Pious Lady Guion, Jeanne Marie Bouvier de La Motte Guyon, 1806

The Good News of God, Charles Kingsley, 1887

The Imitation of Christ, Thomas à Kempis, c.1418

The New Life: Discourses on Christian Experience, Horace Bushnell, 1858

The Sayings of the Desert Fathers, Cistercian Publications, 1975

The Spiritual Meadow, John Moschos, Cistercian Publications, 1992

The Way of Life, Leo Tolstoy, 1910

Theodicy, Essays on the Goodness of God, the Freedom of Man and the Origin of Evil, G.W. Leibniz, 1710

BIBLES CONSULTED

Christian Standard Bible
English Revised Version
English Standard Version
King James Bible
Geneva Bible
Good News Bible
International Standard Version
New American Standard Version
New Catholic Bible
New Century Version
New English Translation
New International Version
New King James Version
New Living Translation
New Revised Standard Version
Revised Geneva Translation
Revised Standard Version
21st Century King James Version

SAINTS AND SINNERS QUOTED

Adelaide Anne Procter, 1825–1864, English poet and hymn writer

Albrecht Dürer, 1471–1528, German Renaissance artist and printmaker

Alcuin, c. 735–804, English scholar and theologian

Alexander Pope, 1688–1744, English poet

Annie Keary, 1825–1879, Irish-English novelist and philanthropist

Saint Anselm, 1033–1109, Italian-born Archbishop of Canterbury - philosopher and theologian

Saint Anthony, c. 251–356, Egyptian hermit

Saint Athanasius, c. 296–373, Egyptian bishop and theologian

Saint Augustine, 354–430, North African bishop and theologian

Saint Basil, c. 330–379, Cappadocian bishop and theologian

Saint Benedict, c. 480–547, Italian monk - founder of Western monasticism

Blaise Pascal, 1623–1662, French mathematician, physicist, and Christian apologist -

Saint Catherine of Siena, 1347–1380, Italian mystic

Charles Kingsley, 1819–1875, English clergyman and novelist

Charles Spurgeon, 1834–1892, English Baptist preacher

Christina Rossetti, 1830–1894, English poet

Saint Columba, c. 521–597, Irish missionary monk

Cranmer, 1489–1556, English theologian and archbishop, author of the *Book of Common Prayer*

Dietrich Bonhoeffer, 1906–1945, German Lutheran pastor and theologian - anti-Nazi resistor, martyr executed by the regime

Dionysius of the ninth century Syrian Jacobite Church, d. 845, Syrian patriarch and historian

Dioscorus, d. 454, Egyptian Pope of Alexandria

E.B. Pusey, 1800–1882, English theologian

Edward E. Hale, 1822–1909, American Unitarian clergyman and writer

Elizabeth Barrett Browning, 1806–1861, English poet

Elizabeth Prentiss, 1818–1878, American hymn writer and novelist

Emily Brontë, 1818–1848, English novelist and poet

Ephrem the Syrian, 4th-century theologian and poet

Esaias Heidenreich, 1532–1589, German Lutheran theologian

Saint Faustina, 1905–1938, Polish nun and mystic

Francis de Sales, 1567–1622, French bishop and mystic

Saint Francis of Assisi, 1181–1226, Italian friar - founder of the Franciscan Order

Pope Francis, 1936-2025, Argentine pope - Jorge Mario Bergoglio

Frederick B. Macnutt, 1873–1949, English Anglican priest and author

George Eliot, 1819–1880, English novelist

George Herbert, 1593–1633, English poet and Anglican priest

George MacDonald, 1824–1905, Scottish minister and writer

Gerard Manley Hopkins, 1844-1889, English poet

Gerhard Tersteegen, 1697–1769, German Reformed mystic and hymn writer

G.K. Chesterton, 1874–1936, English writer and apologist

Gottfried Leibnitz, 1646–1716, German philosopher and mathematician

Gotthold Lessing, 1729–1781, German writer and philosopher

Gregory of Nyssa, 4th-century Eastern Orthodox saint

Madame Guyon, 1648–1717, French mystic

Hadewijch, 13th-century Dutch mystic and poet

Harriet Beecher Stowe, 1811–1896, American novelist

Héloïse d'Argenteuil, 1101-1164, French nun and wife of theologian Peter Abelard

Hildegard von Bingen, 1098–1179, German Benedictine abbess and mystic

Horace Bushnell, 1802–1876, American Congregational theologian

Hryhorii Skovoroda, 1722–1794, Ukrainian philosopher and poet

Immanuel Kant, 1724–1804, German philosopher

Sir Isaac Newton, 1643–1727, English physicist and mathematician

Isaac Watts, 1674–1748, English hymn writer

Jane Austen, 1775–1817, English novelist

J.E. Bode, 1816–1874, English clergyman and hymn translator

Jeremy Taylor, 1613–1667, English cleric and writer, imprisoned by Oliver Cromwell

John Bunyan, 1628–1688, English Puritan writer – author of *The Pilgrim's Progress*

John Chrysostom, c. 347–407, Greek bishop and preacher - known as Chrysostom ('Golden-Mouthed'),

John Henry Newman, 1801–1890, English theologian and cardinal

John Muir, 1838–1914, Scottish-American naturalist and conservationist

St John of The Cross, 1542–1591, Spanish Carmelite mystic

Pope John Paul II, 1920–2005, Polish pope - Karol Wojtyła, long-reigning pontiff

John Pierrpont Greaves, 1777–1842, English mystic and educator

John Ruskin, 1819–1900, English art critic and social thinker

John Wesley, 1703–1791, English cleric and theologian - founder of Methodism

Dr Johnson, 1709–1784, English lexicographer and author

Julian of Norwich, c. 1342–c. 1416, English anchoress and mystic

Lancelot Andrewes, 1555–1626, English bishop and scholar, key translator of the King James Bible

Archbishop Laud, 1573–1645, English archbishop

Leo Tolstoy, 1828–1910, Russian novelist and Christian anarchist - author of *War and Peace* and *Anna Karenina*,

Martin Luther, 1483–1546, German priest and theologian

Mary Anne Kelty, 1799–1873, English writer and devotional author

Saint Patrick, c. 385–461, Romano-British missionary and bishop

Phillips Brooks, 1835–1893, American Episcopal clergyman and hymn writer

Ralph Waldo Emerson, 1803–1882, American essayist and transcendentalist

Richard of Chichester, 1197–1253, English bishop

Samuel Rutherford, 1600–1661, Scottish Presbyterian theologian

Sarah Frances Smiley, 1830–1883, American Quaker

Sarah Williams, 1837–1868, English poet

Simon Weil, 1909-1943, French philosopher

Sojourner Truth, c. 1797–1883, American abolitionist and preacher

Syncletica of Alexandria, c. 270–c. 350, Egyptian desert mother

Saint Teresa Benedicta of the Cross, 1891–1942, German-Jewish philosopher and Carmelite nun

Saint Teresa of Ávila, 1515–1582, Spanish Carmelite nun and mystic

Theodore Studite, 759-826, Byzantine Monk

Saint Thérèse of Lisieux, 1873–1897, French Carmelite nun

Sir Thomas More, 1478–1535, English statesman and martyr

Thomas Merton, 1915-1968, American Trappist monk, writer and theologian

Dr Westcott, 1863–1949, English bishop

William Cowper, 1731–1800, English poet and hymn writer

William Ellery Channing, 1780–1842, American Unitarian clergyman

William Law, 1686–1761, English mystic

ABOUT THE AUTHOR / COMPILER

Joanna Gray read History at Christ Church, Oxford while New Testament theologian The Very Reverend Dr John Drury was Dean. She combines writing and working with children who are unable to attend school. After being confirmed in Gloucester Cathedral, she worships in an ancient parish church in Hampshire, England.

Quadrille, Penguin Random House UK,
One Embassy Gardens, 8 Viaduct Gardens,
London SW11 7BW

Quadrille Publishing Limited is part of the Penguin Random House group of companies whose addresses can be found at global.penguinrandomhouse.com

Penguin Random House UK

Published by Quadrille in 2026

www.penguin.co.uk

A CIP catalogue record for this book is available from the British Library

ISBN 978-1-80712-036-8
10 9 8 7 6 5 4 3 2 1

Managing Editor, Publishing: Sarah Lavelle
Publisher: Kate Pollard
Commissioning Editor: Phoebe Bath
Design: Claire Warner Studio
Illustrator: Lucy Pollard
Head of Production: Stephen Lang
Colour reproduction by p2d

Printed in China by C&C Offset Printing Co., Ltd.

The authorised representative in the EEA is Penguin Random House Ireland, Morrison Chambers, 32 Nassau Street, Dublin D02 YH68.

FSC www.fsc.org MIX Paper FSC® C018179

Penguin Random House is committed to a sustainable future for our business, our readers and our planet. This book is made from Forest Stewardship Council® certified paper.